Contents

I. **CAR COSTS IN FINANCIAL PERSPECTIVE** 1
   Cost Differences Can Be Great 4
   Long-Term Costs vs. Short-Term Savings 5
   Using Consumer Reports 6

II. **RANKING CARS, SPORT UTILITY VEHICLES, SMALL VANS, AND LIGHT PICKUPS BY RESALE VALUE** 9
   Using the Tables 9
   Which Models are Listed 10
   What the Rankings Indicate 11
   Cars:
      Rankings for 2002 Models 15
      Rankings for 2003 Models 19
      Rankings for 2004 Models 22
      Rankings for 2005 Models 26
      Rankings for 2006 Models 30
   Sport Utility Vehicles and Small Vans:
      Rankings for 2002 Models 34
      Rankings for 2003 Models 36
      Rankings for 2004 Models 38
      Rankings for 2005 Models 40
      Rankings for 2006 Models 42
   Light Pickups:
      Rankings for 2002 Models 45
      Rankings for 2003 Models 46
      Rankings for 2004 Models 47
      Rankings for 2005 Models 48
      Rankings for 2006 Models 49

III. **THE AUTOMOBILE PRICE OUTLOOK** 51
   Financing 55
   How to Figure the "Worth"
      of Interest-Rate Differences and Cash Rebates 56
   Hybrids 57
   The Extended Outlook 61

IV. **SHOULD YOU BUY NEW OR USED?** 63
   Useful Information 64
   Used Car Best Buys 65

V. SHOULD YOU BUY OR LEASE? 77
    Understanding a Lease 79
    Comparing Financing Methods 84

VI. SAFETY RECALLS AND LEMON LAWS 87
    Lemon Laws 90

**VII. HOW TO USE
THE N.A.D.A. OFFICIAL USED CAR GUIDE** 93
    Dealer Trade-In or Private Sale? 96

VIII. INSURING YOUR VEHICLE 99
    Auto Insurance Basics 102
    Where to Find Help 109

IX. YOUR COST RECORD 111
    Keeping the Ledgers 111
    Implications of Changes in Component Costs 112
    Calculating Depreciation Costs 113
    Amortize Interest Costs 115

APPENDIX: USEFUL LINKS 117

Monthly Ledger and Annual Summary 119

I.

CAR COSTS IN FINANCIAL PERSPECTIVE

AMERICANS spend more of their disposable incomes on automobiles than on virtually anything else except shelter. But many people—especially younger persons whose first major purchase may well be an automobile—probably have only a vague notion of what the costs of owning and operating a car amount to over the course of their lifetimes, or of how their spending on automobile transportation compares with average U.S. expenditures for transportation and other items, or of how great the eventual costs of seemingly minor luxuries may be in terms of lost educational opportunities, inadequate housing, reduced retirement income—or worse, the inability to acquire needed health care and dignified living conditions during one's later years. Even average car costs probably are far greater than most people suspect.

As shown in Chart 1, Americans spend far more on transportation than they contribute to pensions and Social Security. These outlays—including vehicle purchases, motor fuel, car insurance, maintenance and repairs,

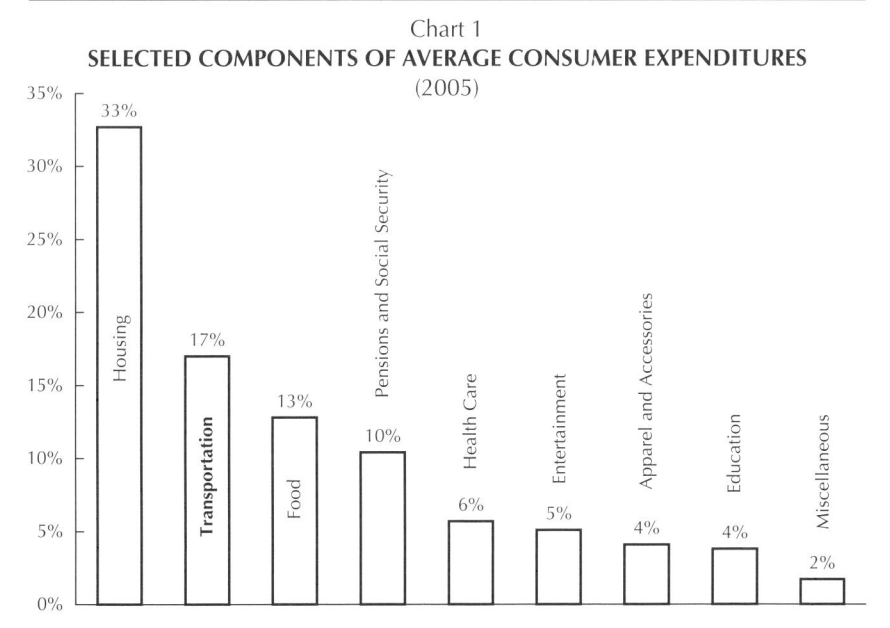

Chart 1
SELECTED COMPONENTS OF AVERAGE CONSUMER EXPENDITURES
(2005)

Category	Percent
Housing	33%
Transportation	17%
Food	13%
Pensions and Social Security	10%
Health Care	6%
Entertainment	5%
Apparel and Accessories	4%
Education	4%
Miscellaneous	2%

Source: *Bureau of Labor Statistics*.

license and registration fees, and more—are more than four times higher than their out-of-pocket outlays for health care or education.

Currently, the estimated average costs of owning and operating a motor vehicle *during the course of an individual's expected driving lifetime*, shown in Table 1, amount to about $300,000, depending on the size of the cars one drives. Consider that this amount represents the costs of owning and driving just one vehicle. Two- and three-car families have proportionally greater costs.

These figures are not given to discourage car ownership—or to imply that anyone who drives anything other than a "clunker" is in some way profligate. On the contrary, for most Americans today automobile transportation is a necessity. Only a small percentage of the workforce lives within walking distance of work, shopping, entertainment, and such. Similarly, for the vast majority of Americans, public transportation either is unavailable, inconvenient, unreliable, or too dangerous to patronize.

Some indication of just how much we rely on cars is given by the fact that currently reported U.S. personal consumption expenditures for "Motor vehicles and parts" plus "user-operated transportation" are about 50 times greater than for "purchased local transportation" via transit systems, taxicabs, and railways. Between 1990 and 2005, the number of registered cars and trucks in the United States increased from 135 million to 240 million,

Table 1
**ESTIMATED AVERAGE COSTS
OF OWNING AND OPERATING AN AUTOMOBILE
IN THE UNITED STATES FOR 50 YEARS**
(Current Dollars)

Cost Category	Small Sedan	Medium Sedan	Large Sedan	4WD Sport Utility Vehicle	Mini-Van
Depreciation	$77,522	$97,878	$127,348	$126,658	$103,218
Gas/Oil	55,500	70,500	75,000	94,500	79,500
Insurance	48,400	47,750	51,600	47,500	44,300
Maintenance	37,500	41,250	46,500	48,000	43,500
Taxes	20,050	27,200	33,400	34,750	29,350
Total:	**$238,972**	**$284,578**	**$333,848**	**$351,408**	**$299,868**

Note: Based on 750,000 miles of travel over 50 years; 12-year, 100 percent depreciation on autos. Source: "Your Driving Costs," American Automobile Association, 2007.

Chart 2
SELECTED COMPONENTS OF THE CONSUMER PRICE INDEX
(1982-84=100)

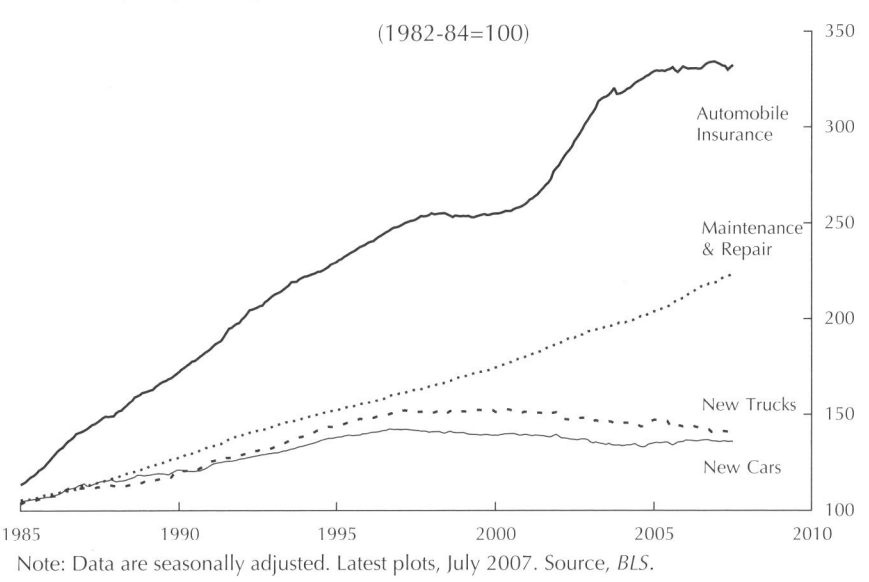

Note: Data are seasonally adjusted. Latest plots, July 2007. Source, *BLS*.

and the number of miles traveled by passenger cars, trucks and motorcycles increased from 2.0 trillion to 2.8 trillion. In 2005, there were 1.2 registered vehicles (automobiles, trucks, buses, and motorcycles) for every licensed driver in the United States.

Since 1990, however, the cost of buying a new vehicle has increased. Between 1990 and 2006, the average consumer expenditure for a new car increased from $15,827 to $24,929.

It is worth noting that this increase is *not* fully reflected in the Consumer Price Index (CPI), the most widely followed barometer of price inflation and price changes. The CPI is designed to measure the change in the price of a "fixed basket" of goods and services—that is, a selected group of items whose quality does not change over time. In fact, the quality of the things we buy *does* change. In particular, the cars we buy today are vastly better than the ones we bought 20 years ago. They are designed and built better, have more features to ensure the comfort and safety of drivers and passengers, require less maintenance, and have better warranties. Often we pay more for these added features. But these additional outlays are not included in the CPI.

When the CPI is calculated, any increase in car prices that is attributable to quality improvements is "netted out." Consequently, even when sticker prices are increasing, the CPI may show that "quality-adjusted" car prices are unchanged or even *decreasing*. This is evident in Chart 2, which shows selected components of the CPI. According to the CPI, the price indexes for new cars and trucks have been decreasing since the late 1990s and increasing modestly since late 2003—even though sticker prices and the amounts that people actually pay when they buy cars have increased.

Other costs of car ownership are easier to measure—and Chart 2 shows that these have increased substantially in the past 20 years. The likelihood of further rises in automobile purchase and ownership costs would seem to make it imperative that car buyers (and other drivers in the family) become clearly aware of the long-term costs of owning and operating different types of cars.

Cost Differences Can Be Great

In this regard, the estimates shown in Table 1 only begin to reveal how great potential cost differences can be. As large as it is, the $112,436 ($351,408- $238,972) estimated difference between driving an SUV and a small sedan over the span of one's driving years ignores several factors that might increase that difference substantially. For example, that estimate omits any consideration of what the amount might accrue to if the annual difference were invested. Assuming that the average annual difference in depreciation over the 12-year "life" of the car ($997 between a large sedan and a small sedan) was invested each year and returned five percent per year, at the end of 50 years, the principal and interest on that investment would amount to $219,052. (At the end of 40 years it also would be a sizable sum, $126,399.) If cars are traded in during the years of their greatest depreciation (the first four years), or if they are purchased on credit instead of cash, then additional cost differences arise.

Consider an extreme hypothetical comparison that takes into account several such factors: that is, the potential investment accrual amounts resulting from the difference between (1) paying cash for the equivalent of today's "average" small sedan and "running it into the ground" before purchasing a similar new replacement for cash, or (2) purchasing a "luxury" automobile on credit with a history of rapid depreciation (see the rankings on pages 15-49) and trading it in every third year on a similar credit purchase of a new "luxury" replacement.

In the first case, average annual costs (in 2007 dollars) based on our estimates would be roughly $4,779. Estimated annual costs (in 2007 dollars) for the "luxury" car, which include depreciation, gas and oil, insurance, taxes and fees, and interest on the car loans amount to about $7, 412. The annual average difference of $2,632, invested each year at five percent, after 50 years would yield about $578,608. After 40 years, the amount would be $333,873—still a substantial sum for use in retirement, for establishing trusts for one's children or grandchildren, or for other purposes.

The purpose of the foregoing illustrations is not to dissuade persons from purchasing luxury cars. Those who can afford such outlays without jeopardizing their other financial interests obviously will do as they choose. Nor should everyone "run their cars into the ground" (however, a number of independent studies have concluded—and we agree—that driving a car as long as possible probably is the most economical practice over the long run).

Clearly, there can be substantial differences in car costs between the extremes given in the examples, and substantial long-term savings can be achieved without the necessity of driving a "junk car" and putting up with the annoyance and inconvenience such cars seem to occasion.

Long-Term Costs vs. Short-Term Savings

This introduction to "car costs" is intended to suggest two points that ought to be obvious but that many people seem to neglect (or were never aware of) when they start shopping for cars: (1) that seemingly minor short-term differences in outlays for auto transportation, say $40 or $50 per month, can become very great differences over the course of 10, 20, 30, or 40 years, and (2) that the long-term savings achieved through informed selections of the most economical cars suited to an individual's or family's needs far outweigh the one-time "savings" of $300 or $400 achieved through "dickering" in the dealer's showroom.

With respect to the first observation, it would seem vitally important not only to the future financial security of many of today's adults, but also to the educational and other long-term prospects of their children, that they make informed choices about cars that acknowledge potential costs to the family's welfare. When they choose a particular costly "option," they should be aware of the longer term sacrifices—either their own or others'—that may be required. Consider, for example, that the estimated cost of four years of tuition, room, and board at a private four-year college now exceeds $120,000. Highly-rated universities cost even more. Or consider that both Social Security and Medicare programs are actuarially unsound and simply will not, in all likelihood, provide benefits to the coming generations of recipients at anywhere near their current levels.

With respect to the second observation, many car buying "guides" tend to emphasize the immediate potential savings to be achieved through a process of informed bargaining in the showroom—which can indeed save you hundreds of dollars. There can be no question that it is important for buyers to ascertain such factors as (1) the actual dealer cost of a car (as opposed to the "sticker price"), (2) what dealer profit margin is acceptable to both buyer and seller, (3) the most economical ways to purchase desired optional equipment, (4) what sales "tricks" to be on the lookout for, (5) how to avoid dealer "add-ons" and "packages" (such as undercoating), (6) how to determine what is a reasonable "trade-in" amount for your old car, and so on.

Using Consumer Reports

These matters have been adequately addressed by other consumer economists—in our view most successfully by those at *Consumer Reports* magazine—and it is needless to try to duplicate their efforts here. Rather, we strongly recommend that car buyers consult the April "Annual Auto Issue" of *Consumer Reports*, back issues of which are available in most public libraries. This issue contains useful information on "how to drive a hard bargain," the results of the magazine's test drives of new models, the reliability ratings of older models, safety test results, and "good bets" and "bad bets" in used cars.

As important as such information unquestionably is for achieving immediate savings, however, it largely ignores matters related to the long-term, and much larger, costs associated with owning and operating a car. Factors relating to what car may be "affordable" for a particular individual or family, or what cars may represent the best long-run *dollar* value, tend to be ignored. In our view, the long-term *financial* aspects of car ownership are just as important as the dealing and mechanical aspects of auto purchasing. Many people have gotten a "good deal" on the purchase of an automobile only to see it repossessed one or two years later (or to find that they must make other substantial financial sacrifices if they are to keep the car). The danger seems to be that in striking what they think is a good bargain, many car buyers are lulled into believing that they have protected their financial interests—when actually they may have committed themselves to long-term outlays that may seriously threaten their financial well-being. That is, many car buyers tend to be "penny-wise and pound-foolish."

An essential first step for individuals and families to take toward adopting a prudent long-term financial perspective with respect to automobile ownership is, very simply, to keep an accurate record of auto transportation costs. This involves more than simply recording car payments, gas purchases and such, and we describe the procedures for accurate record keeping in the section preceding the monthly ledgers (see Chapter IX).

Monitor your costs. Compare them with your expected income, with current and anticipated expenses, and with the data presented here. Then you will be better able to judge at a given time "how much car" is consistent with a prudent family financial plan. If your auto-related expenditures appear much larger in relation to your income than the national averages, then you may be mismanaging your financial affairs—no matter how good the bargain you struck on the purchase price of your car. Such a record also can be a useful tool in alerting other drivers in the family—especially younger people who may not have purchased a car previously—as to the actual amounts involved, which may be far different from what they believe.

II.

RANKING CARS, SPORT UTILITY VEHICLES, SMALL VANS, AND LIGHT PICKUPS BY RESALE VALUE

ONCE you have determined what is an affordable range of car costs, then, obviously, it is in your interest to own and operate a vehicle that provides the best overall value within that range. Again, we strongly advise that you consult carefully the judgments of *Consumer Reports*' automotive specialists as to the roadworthiness and reliability of the models they tested.

There is, however, an additional consideration that ought to enter into the selection of a particular model—one that can result in substantial savings. Not all cars of similar size and original price that have been judged good cars with respect to driving characteristics and engineering features have retained value equally. Some of *Consumer Reports*' "recommended" models have retained much more of their original dollar value than others.

The accompanying tables rank models according to the ratio of average resale prices to manufacturer's suggested retail prices. We have provided these rankings of late-model automobiles as an aid in distinguishing, on the basis of previous resale prices, which models currently seem probable to retain proportionally greater value and which models are more apt to depreciate rapidly.

Using the Tables

The percentages and rankings given in the following tables are derived from the *N.A.D.A. Official Used Car Guide*, September 2007 (see Chapter VII). The resale values listed are an average of the ten regions defined by N.A.D.A.

Cars are listed on pages 15-33. Sport utility vehicles and small vans are listed on pages 34-44, and light pickups are listed on pages 45-49. In each section, three values are given for each automobile:

The ***Original M.S.R.P.*** is the manufacturer's suggested retail price. Unless otherwise indicated, it is based on the lowest-price "bottom of the line" version of each model. That is, it assumes no optional equipment was included.

The ***Retail Value as a Percent of M.S.R.P.*** is the ratio of the average *current* retail value to the *original* M.S.R.P. A high percentage indicates the vehicle has retained relatively more of its value over the years.

Unless otherwise indicated, the M.S.R.P. component of this ratio is based on the lowest-price version of each model. The "NADA retail value" component, however, reflects sales of vehicles that may or may not have optional equipment. Typically, the N.A.D.A. current retail value does *not* include the resale value of expensive options, such as a power sunroof, leather seats, aluminum/alloy wheels, or a premium audio system (the *N.A.D.A. Guide* values these items separately). It *does* include the resale value of less-expensive optional equipment. However, according to N.A.D.A., most optional equipment has little or no value on older vehicles, especially if the options cost relatively little to begin with or are likely to wear with age.

The **Retail Value minus Trade-In** is the difference between the current N.A.D.A. retail value and the N.A.D.A. trade-in value. The trade-in value reflects several adjustments from the retail value, such as the dealer profit margin, deduction for detailing costs, etc.

If you are a *seller*, the retail value minus trade-in is a rough estimate of the difference between what you could expect to realize from a private sale of your car and what a dealer might offer to pay you for it in trade-in. The higher the amount, the more you stand to gain either by selling your car privately, or by bargaining with a dealer to pay you a trade-in price closer to the car's retail price.

If you are a *buyer*, the retail value minus trade-in represents the difference between the retail price a dealer is likely to ask for his used car and the wholesale or trade-in price he might have paid for it. The higher the amount, the more room you have to bargain the price down. This amount also suggests how much bargaining leeway you would have with a private seller, who may ask the retail price but be willing to settle for somewhat less as an alternative to trading it in.

Which Models are Listed

There are hundreds of car and truck models on the road today. A particular vehicle (for example, a 2002 Dodge Stratus) may have been manufactured in a half dozen different models (the V6 Stratus was available as a 2-door SE coupe, a 2-door R/T, a 4-door SE sedan, a 4-door SE Plus, a 4-door ES, and a 4-door R/T).

To keep our lists manageable, we include only base models—with some important exceptions. We include non-base models if their "retail price as a percent of the M.S.R.P." is significantly different from the comparable percentage for the base model. Such differences indicate that a vehicle has depreciated significantly faster or slower than the base model.

What qualifies as a "significantly different" rate of depreciation depends on the model year. For 2004, 2005, and 2006 models, we include a non-base model if the ratio of its retail value to its M.S.R.P. differs from the ratio for the base model by seven percentage points or more. For 2002 and 2003 models, the difference has to be six percentage points or more. The thresholds are smaller for older vehicles because differences in depreciation rates (for different versions of a given model) tend to shrink over time.

An illustration may help. Using these criteria, our list of 2003 cars includes two models of the Audi A4: the 4-cylinder, which is the base model, and the V6. The latter was included because its resale value is significantly lower as a percentage of its M.S.R.P. (60.9 percent) compared with the resale value of the base model (70.1 percent of its M.S.R.P.). Our 2003 list includes only the base model of the Pontiac Grand Am (the four-cylinder SE). The resale prices of the other two V6 Grand Am models, relative to their M.S.R.P.s, were sufficiently close to the base model that they did not merit a separate listing.

Models are most likely to have a significantly different retail value as a percent of M.S.R.P., compared with the base model, if they have a fancier trim package, a more powerful engine, a convertible top, or four-wheel drive. Sometimes these extra features enhance the resale value, relative to the M.S.R.P., but sometimes they reduce it. In other words, a car with premium trim might depreciate faster than the base model, or it might hold its value better. It depends on the model.

In addition, **our tables include every model that *Consumer Reports* has identified as either a "reliable used car" or a "used car to avoid."** In most cases, the editors of *Consumer Reports* do not make a distinction between the base model and other models, but sometimes they do. For example, the 2004 Chrysler Sebring Convertible is tagged by them as a used car to avoid, but the 2004 Sebring Sedan is not.

What the Rankings Indicate

Resale values listed in the *N.A.D.A. Official Used Car Guide* reflect the collective judgments of market participants respecting the overall value of particular makes and models of vehicles. Inasmuch as these judgments are informed by many previous owners' and operators' experiences, they provide a strong indication of how a given make and model has withstood the test of consumer use over an extended period of time.

In some instances, such "market determinations" appear to coincide with the judgments based on evaluations of short duration of one or two "test cars" for a particular model by independent consumer services such as *Consumer Reports*. In other instances, they differ—sometimes very considerably. Admittedly, the usefulness of the accompanying tables is limited by the factors described below. But in the absence of more reliable data, they provide at least some indication of expected performance from similar models now on the market.

The ratios of N.A.D.A. resale values to original manufacturers' suggested retail prices listed in the accompanying tables are not exact measurements of retained dollar value. The manufacturer's suggested retail price (M.S.R.P.) usually is *not* the actual retail sale price of a new car. The actual sale price is always open to negotiation, and in recent years has been subject to even greater fluctuations than usual. Hence, our rankings can be only roughly suggestive.

For some models the original M.S.R.P. used in our tables may understate the actual price that car buyers originally paid. There are two reasons for this. First, the M.S.R.P. reported by the *N.A.D.A. Guide* excludes the cost of major options, but many car buyers do, in fact, purchase these options. Hence, they may pay more than the "base model" M.S.R.P. shown in our tables. This is especially likely with luxury vehicles such as Mercedes and Lexus, which often carry eye-catchingly low M.S.R.P.s for their "entry level" models, but which most customers buy as loaded-up versions at higher prices. Second, some models may sell for more than their M.S.R.P. due to strong demand. When the popular PT Cruiser was introduced a few years ago, some dealers were able to charge $2,000 or more above the sticker price.

The rankings shown in the table probably exaggerate the retained dollar value of such models. This exaggeration is reflected in the fact that the average resale prices for some vehicles, particularly in the later model years, actually exceed their original M.S.R.P. That is, their "retail price as a percent of M.S.R.P." is greater than 100 percent. In fact, these cars probably sold for more than the indicated M.S.R.P. when they were new, and their current resale value almost certainly is less than 100 percent of what they originally sold for.

Conversely, the rankings probably exaggerate the *loss* of dollar value of other cars, namely those which originally sold for less than the M.S.R.P. The M.S.R.P. incorporates a "dealer's profit margin," which differs according to a particular dealer's requirements. This margin may vary substantially from dealer to dealer, depending on such things as carrying costs, availability of some cars, buyer demand, and so on. It is negotiable, and car buyers often pay less than the M.S.R.P. for all but the most popular models.

In recent years, some models have sold for less than the M.S.R.P. for another reason. Car manufacturers, especially the Big Three (GM, Ford, and Chrysler) have been offering very large rebates to new car buyers, sometimes as high as $5,000. Hence, the actual sales price for these vehicles (especially in recent years) may have been substantially less than the M.S.R.P. used to calculate our ratios. The resale value of such vehicles, relative to what they originally sold for, is greater than indicated in the tables. In other words, they have not lost as much value as the tables suggest.

The net effect of these price distortions on our ratios and rankings is impossible to estimate. However, they seem unlikely to change the broad patterns in the rankings. The models that have consistently achieved high resale rankings over the previous seven model years would seem to have a greater prospect of retaining more of their dollar value than do those models that consistently have ranked below the average with respect to resale value.

Two other observations are especially pertinent to the choice of a particular model. First, **different models of roughly similar price and size may have substantially different resale values. When buying a car, if there is a choice to be made between similar size and style cars, and one has been shown in the past to retain substantially greater dollar value than the other, then it is a matter of common sense that the one with the demonstrated higher resale value probably will offer better long-run "value."**

Second, and equally important, some "good" cars with respect to driving characteristics, safety testing, and expected frequency of repair retain less dollar value than other cars judged similarly roadworthy and reliable. The models "recommended" by *Consumer Reports* after "hands-on" testing are indicated by asterisks in the tables. Plainly, some "recommended" models have retained less resale value than other "recommended" models, and even rank lower with respect to retained dollar value than many models that *Consumer Reports* did not recommend. **When buying a car, if there is a choice to be made between two otherwise similar "recommended" cars, it would again seem common sense to pick the one with a record of higher retained dollar value.**

Of course, there is no guarantee that you will end up with a new car that is in every way satisfactory to you, no matter what procedures you follow. Occasionally, even the most promising vehicle turns out to be a "lemon" (see Chapter VI on lemon laws). However, in the absence of some "crystal ball" for predicting the future, taking into account both road-test results and actual resale performance would seem to be a useful way of judging the probable good buys in the automobile market today.

RANKING OF 2002 USED CARS
BY NADA RETAIL VALUE IN SEPTEMBER 2007 AS A PERCENTAGE OF ORIGINAL MANUFACTURER'S SUGGESTED RETAIL VALUE

Rank	Model	Original M.S.R.P.	Retail Value as Percent of M.S.R.P.	Retail Value minus Trade-In
1	Mini Cooper†	$16,300	87.4	$2,141
2	BMW 3 Series*	27,100	77.4	3,110
3	Volkswagen New Beetle†	15,900	72.7	2,042
4	Honda Civic*	12,810	71.6	1,704
5	Toyota Echo*	9,995	70.9	1,516
6	Toyota Celica*	17,085	70.9	2,098
7	Chevrolet Camaro V8	22,295	70.2	2,383
8	Volkswagen Golf†	15,050	69.4	1,834
9	Mercedes-Benz C Class†	24,950	68.6	2,781
10	Honda Accord-4 Cyl.*	15,500	68.4	1,943
11	BMW Z Series*	31,300	67.1	3,108
12	Chevrolet Corvette†	40,805	66.8	3,648
13	Pontiac Firebird V8	25,460	66.4	2,467
14	Acura RSX*	19,950	64.8	2,175
15	Nissan Altima-4 Cyl.*	16,349	64.6	1,937
16	Nissan Sentra	11,799	64.1	1,551
17	Toyota Camry*	18,970	63.8	2,091
18	Volkswagen Jetta†	16,850	63.6	1,945
19	Porsche 911	67,900	62.4	5,223
20	Subaru Impreza*	17,495	61.9	1,877
21	Toyota Camry Solara*	19,365	61.1	2,046
22	Toyota Corolla*	12,568	60.3	1,546
23	Toyota Prius	19,995	59.7	1,983
24	Ford Thunderbird	34,965	59.5	3,160
25	Subaru Legacy-4 Cyl.	19,295	59.0	2,013
26	Lexus IS*	29,435	59.0	2,795
27	Mazda MX-5 Miata*	21,180	58.1	2,119
28	Chevrolet Camaro V6	17,880	57.7	1,916
29	Toyota MR2 Spyder	23,735	57.6	2,225
30	Ford Mustang	17,190	56.9	1,863
31	Mercedes-Benz SLK Class	39,400	56.8	3,225
32	Nissan Altima V6*	22,349	55.9	2,148
33	Saturn S Series*	10,570	55.8	1,397
34	Audi A4†	24,900	55.4	2,311
35	Pontiac Firebird V6	19,515	55.4	1,955
36	Mazda Protégé*	12,955	55.0	1,511
37	Mercedes-Benz CLK Class†	42,550	54.9	3,323
38	Ford Focus†	12,415	54.7	1,503
39	BMW 5 Series	35,950	54.6	2,999
40	Honda S2000*	32,400	54.6	2,560
41	Honda Accord V6*	22,600	54.3	2,109
42	Lexus ES*	31,505	54.3	2,528
43	Honda Insight	19,080	54.2	1,828
44	Porsche Boxster	42,600	54.1	3,298
45	Lexus GS*	38,605	53.3	3,074

RANKING OF 2002 USED CARS
(Continued)

Rank	Model	Original M.S.R.P.	Retail Value as Percent of M.S.R.P.	Retail Value minus Trade-In
46	Subaru Forester	$20,295	53.3	1,965
47	Toyota Avalon*	25,845	51.7	2,274
48	Volkswagen Cabrio†	19,600	51.5	1,884
49	Subaru Legacy-6 Cyl.	27,995	51.4	2,301
50	Subaru Legacy Outback*	27,645	50.5	2,254
51	Audi TT	31,200	49.9	2,656
52	Mercury Cougar V6	17,020	49.7	1,750
53	Lexus SC*	61,055	49.6	4,263
54	Volkswagen Passat†	21,750	49.5	2,088
55	Chrysler PT Cruiser	16,200	49.5	1,718
56	BMW 7 Series†	67,850	49.5	4,561
57	Acura TL	28,880	48.6	2,326
58	Mitsubishi Eclipse*	18,087	48.6	1,776
59	Volvo S60*	27,125	48.4	2,255
60	BMW M5	69,900	47.3	4,533
61	Volvo V70	30,025	47.3	2,344
62	Mitsubishi Lancer	13,897	47.3	1,462
63	Lexus LS*	54,405	47.2	3,918
64	Chevrolet Monte Carlo	19,985	47.1	1,824
65	Infiniti G20*	21,395	47.0	2,025
66	Nissan Maxima	24,699	46.5	2,137
67	Chevrolet Prizm*	14,205	46.5	1,463
68	Acura CL	28,030	46.4	2,250
69	Dodge Neon	12,240	46.2	1,371
70	Saturn L Series†	16,295	44.8	1,657
71	Hyundai Accent†	8,999	44.8	1,202
72	Kia Rio	9,095	44.6	1,213
73	Hyundai Elantra	12,499	44.5	1,361
74	Saab 9-3	27,995	44.2	2,205
75	Mercury Cougar-4 Cyl.	16,520	44.1	1,650
76	Infiniti I35*	28,750	44.0	2,225
77	Chevrolet Impala†	19,885	43.5	1,908
78	Jaguar X-Type†	29,950	43.3	2,391
79	Pontiac Grand Prix†	20,815	43.1	1,784
80	Audi A6†	35,400	43.0	2,622
81	Mercedes-Benz S Class†	71,850	42.4	4,321
82	Pontiac Grand Am†	16,670	42.2	1,638
83	Ford Escort	12,340	41.9	1,320
84	Volvo V40	24,900	41.6	2,050
85	Mercedes-Benz E Class†	48,450	41.5	3,086
86	Pontiac Sunfire	14,465	40.8	1,400
87	Volvo S40	23,900	40.6	1,995
88	Pontiac Bonneville†	25,380	40.2	2,042
89	Volvo C70	37,525	39.7	2,591
90	Mitsubishi Mirage	11,937	39.7	1,271

RANKING OF 2002 USED CARS
(Continued)

Rank	Model	Original M.S.R.P.	Retail Value as Percent of M.S.R.P.	Retail Value minus Trade-In
91	Chrysler Sebring†	$17,705	39.6	1,621
92	Chevrolet Cavalier	13,735	39.6	1,358
93	Suzuki Aerio	13,499	39.5	1,333
94	Chevrolet Malibu†	17,385	39.4	1,598
95	Ford Crown Victoria*	22,755	39.0	1,935
96	Mercury Grand Marquis*	24,085	38.8	1,973
97	Mazda Millenia*	28,025	38.1	2,078
98	Infiniti Q45	50,500	38.1	2,945
99	Mazda 626	18,735	38.0	1,626
100	Oldsmobile Alero†	17,310	37.9	1,575
101	Chrysler 300M	28,340	37.8	2,084
102	Hyundai Sonata	15,499	37.8	1,400
103	Jaguar XK8	69,330	37.7	3,975
104	Mercedes-Benz CL Class†	90,750	37.5	4,553
105	Kia Spectra	10,995	37.4	1,214
106	Lincoln LS	32,795	37.4	2,318
107	Acura RL*	43,150	37.2	2,710
108	Mercedes-Benz SL Class	83,800	37.1	4,360
109	Mercury Sable	19,545	37.0	1,638
110	Dodge Stratus†	17,525	36.9	1,559
111	Mitsubishi Galant	17,707	36.5	1,556
112	Buick Lesabre Custom	24,290	36.1	1,933
113	Ford Taurus	18,635	35.9	1,589
114	Chrysler Concorde	22,370	35.9	1,854
115	Buick Regal LS	23,060	35.8	1,735
116	Jaguar S-Type†	43,675	35.4	2,658
117	Oldsmobile Intrigue	22,667	35.3	1,717
118	Kia Optima	14,899	35.1	1,326
119	Dodge Intrepid	20,570	35.1	1,785
120	Chrysler Sebring Convertible†	25,414	35.0	1,784
121	Buick Century Custom*	20,115	34.9	1,633
122	Suzuki Esteem	13,299	34.2	1,253
123	Audi A8	62,200	34.1	3,549
124	Volvo S80	38,150	34.1	2,404
125	Cadillac Eldorado	41,865	33.5	2,515
126	Mitsubishi Diamante	25,687	33.3	1,907
127	Saab 9-5†	33,995	32.9	2,210
128	Cadillac Deville†	42,125	32.7	2,493
129	Daewoo Lanos	9,199	32.6	1,091
130	Lincoln Town Car*	39,745	32.4	2,381
131	Hyundai XG350	23,999	31.8	1,685
132	Jaguar XJ8	56,330	31.4	2,848
133	Buick Park Avenue	33,270	31.0	2,125
134	Oldsmobile Aurora	30,805	28.9	2,020
135	Daewoo Nubira	11,699	28.1	1,138

RANKING OF 2002 USED CARS
(Continued)

Rank	Model	Original M.S.R.P.	Retail Value as Percent of M.S.R.P.	Retail Value minus Trade-In
136	Cadillac Seville†	$43,524	27.8	2,305
137	Lincoln Continental*	37,760	26.6	2,108
138	Daewoo Leganza	14,599	26.1	1,188

* *Consumer Reports* "reliable used cars." † *Consumer Reports* "used cars to avoid."

RANKING OF 2003 USED CARS
BY NADA RETAIL VALUE IN SEPTEMBER 2007 AS A PERCENTAGE OF ORIGINAL MANUFACTURER'S SUGGESTED RETAIL VALUE

Rank	Model	Original M.S.R.P.	Retail Value as Percent of M.S.R.P.	Retail Value minus Trade-In
1	Mini Cooper†	$16,425	95.6	$2,225
2	Honda Accord-4 Cyl.*	15,800	88.9	2,273
3	Ford Mustang V8†	23,345	87.2	2,776
4	Volkswagen New Beetle†	15,950	87.0	2,250
5	Honda Civic*	12,810	86.8	1,908
6	BMW 3 Series*	27,800	86.3	3,379
7	Volkswagen Golf	15,295	82.3	2,026
8	Toyota Celica*	17,305	82.2	2,285
9	Toyota Echo	10,105	81.6	1,601
10	Mitsubishi Lancer	14,017	79.1	1,809
11	Mercedes-Benz C Class†	24,950	78.6	2,993
12	Toyota Matrix*	14,670	77.6	1,934
13	Toyota Corolla*	13,370	76.3	1,814
14	Volkswagen Jetta†	17,100	75.0	2,148
15	Infiniti G35	27,100	74.9	2,781
16	Saturn Ion†	11,510	74.6	1,642
17	Acura RSX*	19,950	74.1	2,325
18	Chevrolet Corvette	43,225	73.6	4,061
19	Porsche 911†	68,600	73.1	5,770
20	Subaru Impreza*	17,595	72.7	2,037
21	Toyota Camry Solara*	19,365	72.6	2,244
22	Nissan 350Z†	26,269	72.5	2,698
23	Nissan Altima*	16,649	72.1	2,087
24	Toyota Camry*	18,970	71.7	2,239
25	Toyota Prius*	19,995	71.4	2,150
26	Nissan Sentra	12,099	71.2	1,648
27	Subaru Legacy-4 Cyl.*	19,495	70.1	2,235
28	Audi A4-4 Cyl.†	24,950	70.1	2,588
29	Honda Accord V6*	23,000	68.6	2,398
30	BMW Z Series*	33,100	67.7	3,258
31	Pontiac Vibe*	16,340	67.4	1,961
32	Lexus IS*	29,435	67.3	3,026
33	Mazda Protégé*	13,420	67.2	1,694
34	Dodge Neon	12,585	66.7	1,662
35	Audi A6 V8†	47,800	66.7	3,994
36	Mercedes-Benz SLK Class	39,600	66.2	3,583
37	Toyota MR2 Spyder	24,570	65.6	2,425
38	Subaru Forester*	20,545	65.6	2,216
39	Ford Mustang V6	17,475	65.4	2,023
40	Porsche Boxster	42,600	65.3	3,718
41	Subaru Baja*	21,995	65.1	2,296
42	Mercedes-Benz SL Class†	85,990	65.0	6,148
43	Ford Focus	12,680	64.7	1,623
44	BMW 7 Series†	68,500	64.0	5,370
45	Mercedes-Benz CLK Class†	43,900	64.0	3,741

RANKING OF 2003 USED CARS
(Continued)

Rank	Model	Original M.S.R.P.	Retail Value as Percent of M.S.R.P.	Retail Value minus Trade-In
46	Mazda MX-5 Miata	$21,605	63.9	2,249
47	Mercedes-Benz E Class†	46,950	63.6	3,985
48	BMW 3 Series Convertible*	54,500	63.4	4,240
49	Lexus GS*	38,725	63.0	3,448
50	BMW 5 Series	37,600	62.8	3,386
51	Honda Civic Hybrid*	19,550	62.8	1,603
52	Lexus ES*	31,625	62.6	2,760
53	Ford Thunderbird	36,340	62.6	3,273
54	Honda Insight	19,080	62.0	1,978
55	Toyota Avalon*	25,845	61.9	2,466
56	Volvo V70	27,870	61.7	2,535
57	Honda S2000*	32,600	61.5	2,850
58	Cadillac CTS	29,350	61.1	2,833
59	Subaru Impreza WRX*	23,945	60.9	2,163
60	Mazda Mazda6†	18,530	60.9	2,025
61	Audi A4 V6†	31,590	60.9	2,686
62	Volvo S60	26,370	59.4	2,439
63	Subaru Legacy-6 Cyl.*	28,495	58.9	2,461
64	Subara Legacy Outback*	28,008	58.0	2,413
65	Volkswagen Passat†	21,750	57.6	2,215
66	Acura TL	28,980	57.0	2,497
67	Mitsubishi Eclipse	18,137	57.0	1,914
68	Chrysler PT Cruiser†	16,595	56.4	1,822
69	Lexus SC*	62,025	55.5	4,610
70	Audi TT†	32,500	55.4	2,840
71	Acura CL	28,200	55.3	2,444
72	Hyundai Tiburon†	15,999	55.1	1,675
73	Saab 9-3†	25,900	54.5	2,339
74	BMW M5	70,400	54.1	4,998
75	Hyundai Elantra	12,499	54.0	1,483
76	Nissan Maxima	24,899	53.9	2,279
77	Lexus LS*	54,925	53.6	4,210
78	Saturn L Series	17,620	53.6	1,820
79	Infiniti I35*	28,950	53.1	2,430
80	Chevrolet Monte Carlo*	20,465	52.8	1,965
81	Kia Rio	9,250	52.6	1,285
82	Jaguar X-Type	29,305	52.5	2,652
83	Volvo V40	24,900	52.0	2,245
84	Mercedes-Benz S Class	72,600	51.8	4,869
85	Ford ZX2	12,940	51.5	1,475
86	Volvo S40	23,900	51.3	2,190
87	Audi A6 V6†	35,700	50.9	2,874
88	Hyundai Accent	9,749	50.6	1,298
89	Suzuki Aerio†	13,574	50.4	1,485
90	Pontiac Sunfire	14,615	50.1	1,525

RANKING OF 2003 USED CARS
(Continued)

Rank	Model	Original M.S.R.P.	Retail Value as Percent of M.S.R.P.	Retail Value minus Trade-In
91	Pontiac Grand Prix*	$21,505	50.0	1,965
92	Chevrolet Impala	20,465	49.4	2,035
93	Jaguar S-Type†	41,850	49.4	3,063
94	Pontiac Grand Am	17,030	48.8	1,743
95	Mercury Marauder	33,790	48.4	2,485
96	Infiniti Q45	52,000	48.3	3,493
97	Infiniti M45	42,300	48.0	3,128
98	Hyundai Sonata*	15,499	47.5	1,533
99	Mercedes-Benz CL Class	91,650	46.4	5,276
100	Pontiac Bonneville	25,985	46.3	2,168
101	Chevrolet Cavalier	14,025	46.0	1,458
102	Mercury Grand Marquis*	24,070	45.9	2,100
103	Volvo S80	36,455	45.6	2,749
104	Chrysler Sebring†	18,095	45.4	1,728
105	Chevrolet Malibu	17,680	45.2	1,710
106	Jaguar XK8	69,330	45.1	4,369
107	Mercury Sable*	20,120	44.8	1,793
108	Chrysler 300M	28,565	44.7	2,235
109	Acura RL*	43,150	44.3	2,909
110	Kia Spectra†	11,260	43.9	1,292
111	Kia Optima	15,500	43.9	1,480
112	Oldsmobile Alero	17,725	43.8	1,698
113	Ford Crown Victoria*	22,935	43.7	2,025
114	Buick Regal GS*	27,540	43.5	2,073
115	Lincoln Town Car	40,270	42.8	2,790
116	Volvo C70	44,125	42.8	2,893
117	Mitsubishi Galant*	17,767	42.3	1,673
118	Buick Regal LS*	23,595	42.3	1,873
119	Lincoln LS†	33,860	42.3	2,535
120	Dodge Stratus	17,845	41.8	1,668
121	Ford Taurus*	19,180	41.4	1,708
122	Saab 9-5	33,995	40.8	2,496
123	Audi A8	62,200	40.6	3,908
124	Buick Lesabre Custom*	25,020	40.5	2,038
125	Buick Century Custom	20,595	40.2	1,740
126	Hyundai XG350	23,999	39.8	1,833
127	Cadillac Deville†	43,225	39.8	2,786
128	Dodge Intrepid†	20,835	39.7	1,886
129	Chrysler Concorde†	22,860	39.6	1,943
130	Mitsubishi Diamante	25,977	38.8	2,033
131	Jaguar XJ8	56,330	38.0	3,135
132	Buick Park Avenue	33,845	37.6	2,350
133	Oldsmobile Aurora	34,080	37.1	2,345
134	Cadillac Seville†	44,500	34.4	2,633

* *Consumer Reports* "reliable used cars."   † *Consumer Reports* "used cars to avoid."

RANKING OF 2004 USED CARS
BY NADA RETAIL VALUE IN SEPTEMBER 2007 AS A PERCENTAGE OF ORIGINAL MANUFACTURER'S SUGGESTED RETAIL VALUE

Rank	Model	Original M.S.R.P.	Retail Value as Percent of M.S.R.P.	Retail Value minus Trade-In
1	Mini Cooper	$16,449	105.9	$2,316
2	Honda Accord-4 Cyl.*	15,900	99.7	2,400
3	Mitsubishi Lancer	13,022	99.6	1,973
4	Saturn Ion	10,430	99.1	1,845
5	BMW 3 Series	28,100	98.6	3,705
6	Honda Civic*	13,010	97.6	2,038
7	Toyota Echo*	10,245	96.9	1,781
8	Porsche 911*	68,600	96.4	6,819
9	Volkswagen Golf	15,580	94.5	2,157
10	Volkswagen New Beetle†	16,330	93.8	2,357
11	Mazda 3*	13,680	93.7	2,059
12	Toyota Celica	17,390	93.1	2,426
13	Ford Mustang V8	23,245	92.8	2,868
14	Toyota Prius*	19,995	91.5	2,375
15	Mercedes-Benz C Class	25,300	90.7	3,281
16	Toyota Matrix*	14,670	89.5	2,082
17	Subaru Impreza*	17,895	88.5	2,228
18	Scion xB*	13,680	86.9	1,978
19	Scion xA*	12,480	86.1	1,855
20	Toyota Corolla*	13,570	85.5	1,958
21	Nissan 350Z	26,370	85.1	2,984
22	Volkswagen Jetta†	17,430	85.1	2,332
23	Toyota Camry Solara V6*	21,450	84.6	2,572
24	BMW 5 Series†	39,300	84.0	4,128
25	Nissan Sentra†	12,200	83.9	1,820
26	Toyota Camry-4 Cyl.*	18,045	83.1	2,369
27	Infiniti G35*	27,950	82.6	3,062
28	Acura RSX*	20,025	81.8	2,438
29	Audi A4	25,250	81.5	2,810
30	Porsche Boxster†	42,600	81.2	4,238
31	Mercedes-Benz CLK Class†	44,350	80.4	4,342
32	Nissan Altima-4 Cyl.*	16,850	79.0	2,203
33	BMW 6 Series	69,300	79.0	6,054
34	Toyota Camry Solara-4 Cyl.*	19,120	78.5	2,364
35	Lexus IS*	29,435	77.6	3,276
36	Chevrolet Corvette	43,735	77.6	4,204
37	Subaru Legacy-4 Cyl.*	19,895	77.1	2,358
38	Pontiac Vibe*	16,485	77.1	2,148
39	Acura TSX*	26,490	77.0	2,751
40	BMW Z Series	33,600	76.2	3,523
41	Honda Accord V6*	23,300	76.1	2,513
42	Mercedes-Benz SLK Class	39,600	76.0	3,905
43	Toyota Camry V6*	22,260	76.0	2,471
44	Honda Civic Hybrid*	19,500	75.9	2,175
45	BMW 7 Series†	68,500	75.9	5,891

RANKING OF 2004 USED CARS
(Continued)

Rank	Model	Original M.S.R.P.	Retail Value as Percent of M.S.R.P.	Retail Value minus Trade-In
46	Subaru Forester*	$20,895	75.6	2,398
47	Dodge Neon*	13,125	75.5	1,798
48	Subaru Baja	21,995	75.3	2,450
49	Ford Mustang V6	17,720	75.3	2,223
50	Ford Focus	12,725	74.5	1,753
51	Toyota MR2 Spyder	24,645	74.5	2,538
52	Saab 9-3†	26,090	74.1	2,728
53	Honda Insight	19,180	73.9	2,150
54	Volvo S40-5 Cyl.	22,990	73.9	2,525
55	Volkswagen Passat-4 Cyl.	21,780	73.8	2,464
56	Volvo V70*	28,460	73.7	2,863
57	Mercedes-Benz SL Class	88,500	73.7	6,770
58	Acura TL*	32,650	73.6	2,665
59	Nissan Maxima†	26,950	73.5	2,756
60	Lexus ES*	31,725	72.9	3,020
61	Lexus GS*	38,725	72.3	3,683
62	Mazda MX-5 Miata*	21,868	71.5	2,391
63	Mercedes-Benz E Class†	47,450	71.1	4,237
64	Volvo S60	26,960	71.0	2,676
65	Toyota Avalon*	26,045	70.2	2,598
66	Subaru Impreza WRX*	26,495	69.9	2,374
67	Mitsubishi Eclipse	17,702	69.8	2,107
68	Nissan Altima V6*	22,750	69.7	2,408
69	Audi S4	45,650	69.6	3,710
70	Honda S2000*	32,800	69.1	3,000
71	Subaru Legacy-6 Cyl.*	27,095	69.0	2,589
72	Ford Thunderbird†	36,925	68.8	3,495
73	Mazda RX-8-Rotary†	25,180	67.4	2,523
74	Mazda 6†	18,750	67.3	2,150
75	Hyundai Tiburon	16,999	67.0	1,948
76	Cadillac CTS V6	30,140	66.9	3,048
77	Chevrolet Aveo†	11,150	66.1	1,538
78	Lexus LS*	55,125	65.2	4,700
79	Subaru Legacy Outback*	28,025	64.7	2,558
80	Saturn L Series L4	16,370	64.6	1,918
81	Lexus SC*	62,575	64.4	5,113
82	Kia Rio	9,740	64.3	1,431
83	Jaguar X-Type†	29,330	63.3	2,661
84	Hyundai Accent	9,999	63.1	1,442
85	Audi TT	33,250	62.8	3,093
86	Chrysler PT Cruiser†	17,395	62.3	1,957
87	Volkswagen Passat V6†	29,780	62.1	2,630
88	Suzuki Aerio	12,999	62.0	1,596
89	Hyundai Elantra*	13,299	61.6	1,598
90	Chevrolet Monte Carlo*	21,165	61.3	2,159

RANKING OF 2004 USED CARS
(Continued)

Rank	Model	Original M.S.R.P.	Retail Value as Percent of M.S.R.P.	Retail Value minus Trade-In
91	Chevrolet Impala	$21,240	61.2	2,249
92	Audi A6 V6	35,950	61.0	3,201
93	Mercedes-Benz S Class†	73,600	60.8	5,413
94	Mitsubishi Galant†	17,402	60.8	1,915
95	Pontiac GTO†	31,795	59.5	2,625
96	Kia New Spectra	12,620	59.4	1,540
97	Infiniti I35*	30,600	59.1	2,583
98	Suzuki Forenza	12,499	58.5	1,531
99	Saturn L Series V6	20,785	58.4	2,101
100	Chrysler Sebring V6†	19,850	58.2	2,033
101	Cadillac CTS V8	49,300	57.6	3,773
102	Pontiac Grand Prix*	21,760	57.6	2,133
103	Jaguar S-Type†	43,230	57.0	3,422
104	Infiniti Q45	52,400	57.0	3,914
105	Volvo V40	25,450	56.6	2,355
106	Volvo C70†	39,880	56.5	3,260
107	Cadillac XLR	75,385	56.3	5,290
108	Jaguar XK8	69,330	55.9	4,956
109	Volkswagen Phaeton	64,600	55.8	4,376
110	Volvo S40-4 Cyl.	24,450	55.8	2,295
111	Mercury Marauder	33,770	55.7	2,625
112	Pontiac Sunfire	14,930	55.7	1,600
113	Infiniti M45	43,250	55.2	3,348
114	Pontiac Bonneville	26,845	55.1	2,377
115	Kia Spectra	11,820	55.1	1,463
116	Pontiac Grand Am SE-4 Cyl.	17,070	54.5	1,813
117	Jaguar XJ8	59,330	54.5	4,078
118	Volvo S80*	35,450	54.5	2,991
119	Chevrolet Cavalier	14,045	54.2	1,550
120	Mercedes-Benz CL Class	92,800	53.3	5,729
121	Saab 9-5	32,200	53.3	2,781
122	Audi A6 V8	46,950	52.9	3,404
123	Hyundai Sonata*	15,999	52.8	1,608
124	Mercury Grand Marquis*	23,970	52.6	2,218
125	Chrysler Crossfire†	33,620	52.3	2,550
126	Audi A8†	68,500	52.2	4,683
127	Chrysler Sebring-4 Cyl.	18,605	52.2	1,851
128	Chevrolet Malibu†	18,370	52.2	1,825
129	Chrysler 300M	29,185	52.0	2,418
130	Suzuki Verona	16,499	51.6	1,626
131	Acura RL*	43,255	51.0	3,230
132	Kia Optima	15,500	50.9	1,575
133	Lincoln LS†	31,860	50.9	2,720
134	Oldsmobile Alero	20,865	50.2	1,925
135	Buick Regal LS*	24,235	50.0	2,105

RANKING OF 2004 USED CARS
(Continued)

Rank	Model	Original M.S.R.P.	Retail Value as Percent of M.S.R.P.	Retail Value minus Trade-In
136	Hyundai XG350	$23,999	49.4	2,080
137	Lincoln Town Car*	41,020	49.4	3,058
138	Mercury Sable*	20,925	48.7	1,899
139	Mitsubishi Diamante	24,999	48.6	2,186
140	Oldsmobile Alero	18,200	48.0	1,775
141	Dodge Stratus	18,420	47.9	1,780
142	Kia Amanti	24,995	47.9	2,080
143	Pontiac Grand Am SE V6	20,585	47.4	1,848
144	Ford Taurus*	19,660	47.2	1,814
145	Ford Crown Victoria*	23,620	46.4	2,095
146	Chrysler Concorde	23,480	45.9	2,083
147	Buick Lesabre Custom*	25,745	45.9	2,158
148	Cadillac Deville	44,650	45.8	3,086
149	Buick Park Avenue	34,750	45.8	2,700
150	Dodge Intrepid	21,385	45.2	1,998
151	Chevrolet Classic	18,755	44.5	1,748
152	Buick Century Custom*	22,430	44.2	1,870
153	Cadillac Seville	45,535	39.2	2,825

* *Consumer Reports* "reliable used cars."   † *Consumer Reports* "used cars to avoid."

RANKING OF 2005 USED CARS
BY NADA RETAIL VALUE IN SEPTEMBER 2007 AS A PERCENTAGE OF ORIGINAL MANUFACTURER'S SUGGESTED RETAIL VALUE

Rank	Model	Original M.S.R.P.	Retail Value as Percent of M.S.R.P.	Retail Value minus Trade-In
1	Mitsubishi Lancer	$13,999	129.8	$2,343
2	Mini Cooper	16,449	124.3	2,478
3	Toyota Echo*	10,355	110.3	1,950
4	Porsche 996 911†	76,000	109.9	7,908
5	Honda Civic*	13,160	109.1	2,150
6	Honda Accord-4 Cyl.*	16,195	107.0	2,494
7	Mazda 3*	13,680	106.8	2,167
8	BMW 3 Series*	29,300	105.6	3,952
9	Volkswagen New Beetle†	16,570	104.8	2,502
10	Mercedes-Benz C Class	25,850	103.6	3,618
11	Toyota Celica	17,670	103.4	2,538
12	Toyota Matrix*	14,760	101.3	2,183
13	Porsche 997 911	69,300	101.3	7,109
14	Subaru Impreza*	17,995	101.0	2,368
15	Saturn Ion†	11,430	100.8	1,954
16	Mini Cooper Convertible†	20,950	98.2	2,478
17	Volkswagen Golf	15,830	97.6	2,211
18	Nissan 350Z	26,500	95.9	3,233
19	Toyota Corolla*	13,680	95.6	2,078
20	Audi A4-4 Cyl.	25,800	95.2	3,139
21	Chevrolet Corvette†	43,445	95.0	4,753
22	Nissan Sentra	12,500	94.2	1,960
23	Mercedes-Benz SLK Class†	45,500	94.0	4,838
24	Audi A4-4 Cyl.	27,350	93.9	3,263
25	Toyota Prius*	20,875	93.8	2,425
26	Scion xB*	13,680	93.8	2,055
27	Scion tC	15,950	93.3	2,175
28	Chrysler PT Cruiser	13,405	93.2	2,118
29	Scion xA*	12,480	93.2	1,968
30	Volkswagen Jetta†	17,680	92.3	2,420
31	Porsche Boxster	43,800	92.0	4,698
32	BMW 5 Series†	41,300	91.7	4,518
33	Mercedes-Benz CLK Class†	45,250	91.6	4,749
34	Acura RSX*	20,175	91.4	2,556
35	Toyota Camry-4 Cyl.*	18,045	90.5	2,439
36	Toyota Avalon*	26,350	90.5	3,095
37	Chevrolet Aveo†	9,455	90.3	1,630
38	Subaru Legacy-4 Cyl.*	20,995	90.2	2,614
39	Toyota Camry Solara V6*	21,550	89.6	2,634
40	Ford Mustang†	18,560	89.5	2,454
41	Chrysler 300†	22,970	89.5	2,822
42	BMW M3†	47,300	89.4	4,845
43	Audi A4 V6	31,950	88.3	3,460
44	Chevrolet Cobalt	13,625	86.9	1,992
45	Subaru Baja*	22,095	86.9	2,623

RANKING OF 2005 USED CARS
(Continued)

Rank	Model	Original M.S.R.P.	Retail Value as Percent of M.S.R.P.	Retail Value minus Trade-In
46	Volvo S40	$23,260	86.7	2,803
47	Lexus IS	29,435	86.7	3,514
48	Acura TSX*	26,990	86.4	2,903
49	Dodge Neon*	13,615	86.1	1,966
50	BMW 6 Series	69,900	86.0	6,418
51	Volvo V70	28,760	85.9	3,169
52	Mercedes-Benz E Class†	48,500	85.8	4,843
53	Subaru Forester*	21,195	85.6	2,533
54	Audi S4 V8	46,100	85.5	4,291
55	Audi A6	40,250	85.3	4,229
56	BMW Z Series	34,300	85.2	3,839
57	Honda Civic Hybrid*	19,650	85.1	2,280
58	Infiniti G35*	30,450	85.0	3,264
59	Nissan Altima*	17,250	85.0	2,324
60	Honda Insight	19,330	85.0	2,270
61	Lexus ES*	31,975	84.7	3,395
62	Acura TL*	32,900	84.2	3,428
63	Saab 9-3	26,850	84.2	2,992
64	Toyota Camry V6*	22,380	84.0	2,598
65	BMW 7 Series†	69,900	83.7	6,330
66	Honda Accord V6*	23,800	83.7	2,690
67	Hyundai Accent*	9,999	83.4	1,607
68	Pontiac Vibe*	16,915	83.2	2,272
69	Audi A4 V6	35,400	83.1	3,528
70	Toyota Camry Solara-4 Cyl.*	19,220	83.0	2,415
71	Mercedes-Benz SL Class†	89,900	83.0	7,368
72	Ford Focus	13,005	82.9	1,878
73	Volvo S60*	27,235	82.7	2,986
74	Audi S4	45,850	82.7	4,212
75	Kia Rio	9,740	81.8	1,576
76	Volkswagen Passat-4 Cyl.†	22,070	81.2	2,605
77	Lexus GS	38,875	80.8	4,001
78	Volvo V50	25,660	80.2	2,825
79	Hyundai Tiburon	15,999	80.2	2,058
80	Subaru Impreza WRX*	27,095	79.9	2,568
81	Nissan Maxima	27,100	78.7	2,923
82	Lexus LS*	55,675	78.3	5,358
83	Mazda MX-5 Miata*	22,098	77.8	2,481
84	Chrysler Crossfire†	29,045	77.3	3,070
85	Toyota MR2 Spyder	25,145	77.0	2,600
86	Lexus SC*	63,175	76.5	5,685
87	Hyundai Elantra*	13,299	76.3	1,806
88	Mazda RX-8-Rotary	25,375	76.2	2,715
89	Cadillac CTS V6	30,000	75.8	3,273
90	Mazda 6	18,995	75.4	2,309

RANKING OF 2005 USED CARS
(Continued)

Rank	Model	Original M.S.R.P.	Retail Value as Percent of M.S.R.P.	Retail Value minus Trade-In
91	Kia Spectra	$12,620	75.4	1,744
92	Audi TT	33,500	75.3	3,499
93	Jaguar X-Type†	30,330	75.2	3,117
94	Mitsubishi Eclipse	19,449	75.1	2,311
95	Ford Thunderbird	37,460	74.8	3,748
96	Honda S2000*	32,950	74.4	3,100
97	Jaguar XJ8†	60,830	73.7	5,402
98	Dodge Magnum†	21,870	73.1	2,465
99	Acura RL	48,165	72.5	4,264
100	Subaru Legacy-6 Cyl.*	30,995	72.4	2,858
101	Subaru Legacy Outback*	29,212	71.8	2,761
102	Suzuki Aerio	13,449	71.7	1,749
103	Mercedes-Benz S Class	75,300	70.6	5,955
104	Honda Accord Hybrid*	30,990	69.8	2,814
105	Ford Five Hundred	22,145	69.5	2,378
106	Pontiac GTO	32,295	69.5	2,975
107	Volkswagen Phaeton	66,950	68.9	5,041
108	Saab 9-2X*	22,990	68.4	2,400
109	Mitsubishi Galant	18,699	68.1	2,161
110	Pontiac G6	20,675	67.8	2,270
111	Cadillac STS	40,300	67.3	3,693
112	Buick Lacrosse*	22,835	67.0	2,358
113	Volkswagen Passat V6	29,790	67.0	2,766
114	Audi A8 V8†	66,590	66.7	5,408
115	Chevrolet Impala	22,120	66.7	2,371
116	Jaguar S-Type†	44,230	66.6	3,850
117	Pontiac Grand Prix*	22,800	66.3	2,343
118	Chrysler Sebring V6	20,070	66.0	2,189
119	Suzuki Forenza	13,449	65.8	1,663
120	Hyundai Sonata*	15,999	65.3	1,835
121	Mercury Montego	24,345	65.2	2,413
122	Volvo S80*	35,900	65.1	3,314
123	Chevrolet Monte Carlo	22,050	65.1	2,275
124	Mercedes-Benz CL Class	93,900	64.6	6,495
125	Saab 9-5	32,550	64.4	3,106
126	Jaguar XK8	69,830	64.1	5,417
127	Cadillac CTS V8	49,300	64.0	4,073
128	Suzuki Reno	13,449	63.7	1,650
129	Pontiac Sunfire	15,015	63.7	1,725
130	Chevrolet Cavalier	14,325	63.0	1,695
131	Cadillac XLR	75,835	62.6	5,575
132	Dodge Stratus V6	19,995	62.2	2,106
133	Saturn L Series	21,370	61.9	2,193
134	Pontiac Bonneville†	27,650	60.6	2,546
135	Infiniti Q45	55,900	59.8	4,179

RANKING OF 2005 USED CARS
(Continued)

Rank	Model	Original M.S.R.P.	Retail Value as Percent of M.S.R.P.	Retail Value minus Trade-In
136	Kia Optima	$15,900	59.3	1,741
137	Kia Amanti	24,995	58.5	2,350
138	Hyundai XG350	24,399	58.1	2,288
139	Mercury Grand Marquis	24,370	57.8	2,334
140	Chrysler Sebring-4 Cyl.	19,350	57.3	1,990
141	Mercury Sable*	20,855	57.2	2,069
142	Lincoln Town Car*	41,675	57.1	3,341
143	Chevrolet Malibu	18,995	56.6	1,925
144	Suzuki Verona	17,449	56.4	1,783
145	Lincoln LS†	32,330	55.7	2,843
146	Dodge Stratus-4 Cyl.	19,145	55.3	1,938
147	Ford Taurus*	20,485	54.8	2,006
148	Buick Century*	21,945	53.3	2,038
149	Cadillac Deville	45,600	52.9	3,406
150	Buick Park Avenue	35,555	52.5	2,875
151	Pontiac Grand Am	19,870	52.4	1,900
152	Buick Lesabre Custom*	26,425	52.2	2,300
153	Ford Crown Victoria	24,085	51.2	2,201
154	Chevrolet Classic	19,505	49.6	1,833
155	Buick Century Custom*	22,870	48.9	2,025

* *Consumer Reports* "reliable used cars." † *Consumer Reports* "used cars to avoid."

RANKING OF 2006 USED CARS
BY NADA RETAIL VALUE IN SEPTEMBER 2007 AS A PERCENTAGE OF ORIGINAL MANUFACTURER'S SUGGESTED RETAIL VALUE

Rank	Model	Original M.S.R.P.	Retail Value as Percent of M.S.R.P.	Retail Value minus Trade-In
1	Mitsubishi Lancer	$14,599	130.1	$2,420
2	BMW 3 Series	30,300	124.2	4,482
3	Honda Civic*	14,360	120.9	2,318
4	Chevrolet Corvette†	43,800	119.6	5,493
5	Mazda 3*	13,710	119.2	2,260
6	Pontiac Solstice†	19,420	113.6	2,836
7	Subaru Impreza*	18,295	113.1	2,501
8	BMW Z Series	35,600	112.6	4,661
9	Lexus IS*	29,990	111.9	4,191
10	Saturn Ion	11,925	111.3	2,115
11	Porsche 911†	71,300	110.4	7,627
12	Toyota Matrix*	15,110	110.2	2,279
13	Volkswagen Rabbit	14,990	108.5	2,255
14	Mercedes-Benz C Class†	29,200	107.7	4,017
15	Audi A4-4 Cyl. Turbo	27,640	107.6	3,564
16	Toyota Corolla*	14,005	105.8	2,179
17	Mercedes-Benz SLK Class	42,900	105.6	5,023
18	Volkswagen New Beetle	18,390	105.4	2,600
19	BMW 7 Series†	70,500	105.3	7,338
20	Mercedes-Benz CLK Class†	45,750	104.8	5,185
21	Honda Accord-4 Cyl.*	18,225	104.8	2,624
22	Volkswagen Golf	16,030	104.1	2,281
23	BMW 6 Series	71,800	104.1	7,380
24	Chevrolet Aveo	9,455	103.9	1,765
25	Nissan Sentra†	13,100	102.1	2,083
26	Scion xB*	13,880	101.9	2,150
27	Mercedes-Benz CLS Class†	64,900	101.9	6,829
28	BMW 5 Series†	41,800	101.5	4,824
29	Volvo S40†	23,755	101.3	3,124
30	Nissan 350Z*	27,450	101.0	3,415
31	Volvo C70	38,710	100.9	4,600
32	Porsche Boxster†	45,000	100.3	5,000
33	Chrysler PT Cruiser†	14,210	99.9	2,267
34	Acura RSX†	20,325	99.6	2,691
35	Audi A4 V6	33,940	99.4	3,873
36	Scion xA	12,730	99.3	2,050
37	Chevrolet Cobalt	13,900	99.0	2,127
38	Dodge Charger†	18,939	98.7	2,660
39	Scion tC*	16,200	98.1	2,233
40	Toyota Prius*	21,725	97.9	2,525
41	Ford Mustang†	19,115	97.8	2,605
42	Audi S4	46,400	97.7	4,701
43	Toyota Avalon*	26,625	97.5	3,288
44	Mercedes-Benz E Class	50,050	97.4	5,319
45	Toyota Camry Solara V6*	21,710	97.4	2,763

RANKING OF 2006 USED CARS
(Continued)

Rank	Model	Original M.S.R.P.	Retail Value as Percent of M.S.R.P.	Retail Value minus Trade-In
46	Chrysler 300 V6	$23,525	97.1	3,003
47	Volkswagen Jetta	17,900	96.9	2,490
48	Honda Insight	19,330	96.5	2,398
49	Mazda MX-5 Miata	20,435	96.4	2,653
50	Kia Rio	10,570	96.1	1,818
51	Volvo V70*	29,445	95.2	3,432
52	Toyota Camry-4 Cyl.*	18,445	95.2	2,503
53	Audi A3	24,740	94.9	3,042
54	Subaru Legacy-4 Cyl.*	21,695	94.8	2,713
55	Pontiac Vibe*	16,430	94.6	2,400
56	Subaru Baja	22,495	94.4	2,793
57	Lexus ES*	32,300	94.3	3,593
58	Volvo V50†	26,205	93.8	3,153
59	Pontiac G6 V6	20,030	93.7	2,600
60	Mercedes-Benz S Class	64,900	93.7	6,479
61	Infiniti M35*	40,100	93.7	4,469
62	Porsche Cayman	58,900	93.1	5,648
63	Mitsubishi Eclipse*	19,399	92.5	2,525
64	Nissan Altima-4 Cyl.†	17,650	92.4	2,438
65	Subaru Forester*	21,795	92.4	2,684
66	Volkswagen GTI	21,990	92.0	2,473
67	Jaguar XJ8	61,830	92.0	6,227
68	Acura TSX*	27,890	91.9	3,096
69	Lexus GS300	42,900	91.7	4,614
70	Mercedes-Benz SL Class	92,900	91.7	8,033
71	Lexus LS*	56,525	91.4	5,853
72	Acura TL*	33,325	91.4	3,628
73	Chrysler 300 V8†	33,425	91.4	3,733
74	Audi A6 V6	40,820	91.4	4,483
75	Honda Civic Hybrid	21,850	91.0	2,450
76	Infiniti G35*	31,050	91.0	3,481
77	Ford Fusion-4 Cyl.*	17,145	90.7	2,398
78	Hyundai Elantra*	13,675	90.6	2,026
79	Nissan Altima V6*	23,500	90.3	2,793
80	Ford Focus†	13,450	90.2	2,003
81	Hyundai Tiburon	16,095	90.1	2,153
82	Infiniti M45*	46,950	90.0	4,843
83	Saab 9-3†	25,900	89.6	3,033
84	BMW M5	81,200	89.6	7,253
85	Toyota Camry V6*	22,780	89.1	2,710
86	Toyota Camry Solara-4 Cyl.*	19,380	89.1	2,486
87	Honda Accord V6*	25,100	89.1	2,852
88	Hyundai Accent	12,455	88.9	1,925
89	Volkswagen Passat-4 Cyl.†	22,950	88.4	2,795
90	Subaru Impreza WRX*	26,620	88.0	2,651

RANKING OF 2006 USED CARS
(Continued)

Rank	Model	Original M.S.R.P.	Retail Value as Percent of M.S.R.P.	Retail Value minus Trade-In
91	Jaguar X-Type	$32,330	88.0	3,621
92	Lexus GS430	51,125	88.0	4,978
93	Jaguar S-Type	45,330	87.8	4,620
94	Chevrolet HHR	15,425	87.7	2,213
95	Mercury Milan-4 Cyl.*	18,345	87.6	2,420
96	Volvo S60 (FWD)*	30,270	87.2	3,321
97	Mazda 5	17,435	87.2	2,376
98	Dodge Magnum V8	30,235	86.6	3,348
99	Kia Spectra	12,895	85.8	1,904
100	Hyundai Azera*	24,335	85.0	2,766
101	Lincoln Zephyr*	28,995	84.5	3,378
102	Volkswagen Phaeton	66,700	84.5	5,763
103	Saab 9-2X	22,990	84.4	2,649
104	Mazda RX-8-Rotary	26,435	84.2	2,953
105	Mazda 6	19,110	84.1	2,421
106	Audi A6 V8	53,770	83.8	4,988
107	Lexus SC	65,355	83.6	6,085
108	Subaru Legacy-6 Cyl.*	28,995	83.3	2,969
109	Ford Fusion V6*	20,625	82.7	2,475
110	Cadillac CTS V6	30,515	82.6	3,498
111	Mercury Milan V6*	21,345	81.5	2,499
112	Chrysler Crossfire	29,145	81.5	3,094
113	Mazda Speed6	27,995	81.2	2,873
114	Nissan Maxima	27,750	81.2	2,986
115	Audi TT	33,990	81.2	3,719
116	Cadillac XLR	76,480	81.2	6,584
117	Saab 9-5	33,975	81.0	3,719
118	Audi A8 V8	68,130	80.7	6,108
119	Buick Lucerne*	26,265	80.2	2,831
120	Pontiac G6-4 Cyl	17,365	80.1	2,238
121	Acura RL	48,565	79.9	4,583
122	Dodge Magnum V6	22,320	79.9	2,571
123	Honda S2000	34,050	79.7	3,400
124	Suzuki Aerio	13,999	79.4	1,911
125	Cadillac DTS*	41,195	79.4	4,076
126	Cadillac STS†	41,020	78.9	4,114
127	Pontiac GTO	32,295	78.9	3,283
128	Mercedes-Benz CL Class	95,500	78.5	7,393
129	Subaru Legacy Outback*	29,881	77.2	2,887
130	Chevrolet Impala V8*	27,130	76.7	2,893
131	Ford Five Hundred	22,230	76.5	2,472
132	Honda Accord Hybrid*	31,990	75.9	2,951
133	Volvo S80*	37,585	75.8	3,775
134	Pontiac Grand Prix†	22,435	75.6	2,475
135	Hyundai Sonata	17,895	74.2	2,098

RANKING OF 2006 USED CARS
(Continued)

Rank	Model	Original M.S.R.P.	Retail Value as Percent of M.S.R.P.	Retail Value minus Trade-In
136	Suzuki Reno	$13,199	74.1	1,775
137	Buick Lacrosse*	22,935	73.7	2,465
138	Mitsubishi Galant	19,399	73.6	2,288
139	Chevrolet Malibu	17,365	73.0	2,148
140	Mercury Montego	24,430	72.1	2,505
141	Suzuki Forenza	13,699	72.0	1,781
142	Kia Optima-4 Cyl.	16,195	70.3	1,930
143	Cadillac STS V-Series V8	74,270	70.0	5,873
144	Cadillac CTS V8	50,675	69.8	4,298
145	Audi A8 W12	118,190	69.8	7,858
146	Chevrolet Monte Carlo	21,330	69.8	2,333
147	Lincoln Town Car†	42,055	65.4	3,681
148	Lincoln LS	39,285	65.3	3,565
149	Mercury Grand Marquis†	24,780	65.0	2,466
150	Suzuki Verona	18,299	64.5	1,978
151	Kia Optima V6	18,995	64.5	2,014
152	Chrysler Sebring	19,705	63.9	2,130
153	Kia Amanti	27,795	60.9	2,470
154	Chevrolet Impala V6	21,330	60.4	1,979
155	Ford Taurus	20,830	58.4	2,099
156	Dodge Stratus	20,465	56.9	2,050
157	Ford Crown Victoria†	24,510	49.8	1,975
158	Jaguar XK8	69,830	37.4	2,941

* *Consumer Reports* "reliable used cars." † *Consumer Reports* "used cars to avoid."

RANKING OF 2002 USED SPORT UTILITY VEHICLES AND SMALL VANS
BY NADA RETAIL VALUE IN SEPTEMBER 2007 AS A PERCENTAGE OF ORIGINAL MANUFACTURER'S SUGGESTED RETAIL VALUE

Rank	Model	Original M.S.R.P.	Retail Value as Percent of M.S.R.P.	Retail Value minus Trade-In
1	Jeep Wrangler	$15,230	86.1	$2,175
2	Toyota RAV4*	16,525	82.1	2,220
3	Volkswagen Eurovan†	26,200	71.5	2,797
4	Honda CR-V*	18,800	69.1	2,167
5	Nissan Xterra-V6*	19,199	66.8	2,299
6	Jeep Liberty	16,450	66.0	2,135
7	Toyota 4Runner*	26,335	63.4	2,631
8	BMW X5-I6	38,900	61.1	3,335
9	Toyota Highlander*	23,880	59.0	2,281
10	Toyota Sequoia	31,265	58.6	2,761
11	Lexus RX300*	33,955	56.6	2,810
12	Saturn Vue†	16,106	55.2	1,954
13	Nissan Xterra-4 Cyl.*	17,999	54.2	2,040
14	Honda Odyssey	24,250	53.8	2,323
15	Ford Excursion	34,950	53.6	2,804
16	Hyundai Santa Fe*	17,199	53.0	1,980
17	Acura MDX*	34,700	52.1	2,715
18	Ford Escape	18,205	51.6	2,007
19	Mercedes-Benz M Class†	36,300	50.5	2,730
20	Toyota Sienna*	23,905	49.3	2,206
21	Mazda Tribute-V6	20,635	49.2	2,076
22	Suzuki Grand Vitara*	18,599	48.8	1,977
23	Chevrolet Tahoe	32,364	48.7	2,564
24	Mitsubishi Montero	22,217	48.4	2,122
25	Nissan Pathfinder	26,649	48.1	2,298
26	Cadillac Escalade	47,290	48.1	3,125
27	Suzuki XL-7	19,599	48.0	2,007
28	Toyota Land Cruiser*	52,595	47.9	3,278
29	Ford Explorer†	21,135	47.9	2,067
30	Lexus LX470*	61,855	47.7	3,835
31	Chevrolet Trailblazer-I6†	25,155	47.5	2,230
32	GMC Yukon	33,252	47.4	2,564
33	BMW X5-V8†	66,200	46.5	3,923
34	Chevrolet Tracker*	15,865	46.3	1,808
35	Chevrolet Suburban	35,098	46.3	2,598
36	Honda Passport†	23,300	46.3	2,128
37	Mazda MPV	22,250	46.2	2,088
38	Isuzu Rodeo Sport	16,100	45.5	1,803
39	Suzuki Vitara	15,599	45.4	1,783
40	Infiniti QX4*	34,150	44.8	2,545
41	Nissan Quest	22,739	44.8	2,085
42	GMC Denali	43,385	44.3	2,808
43	Jeep Grand Cherokee†	25,425	43.7	2,155
44	GMC Envoy†	28,820	43.6	2,278
45	Chrysler Voyager†	16,355	43.3	1,781

RANKING OF 2002 USED SPORT UTILITY VEHICLES AND SMALL VANS
(Continued)

Rank	Model	Original M.S.R.P.	Retail Value as Percent of M.S.R.P.	Retail Value minus Trade-In
46	Mazda Tribute-4 Cyl.	$18,155	42.7	1,850
47	Chevrolet Blazer†	19,195	42.5	1,888
48	Buick Rendezvous†	24,924	42.4	2,111
49	Ford Expedition	30,195	42.4	2,294
50	Mercury Villager	19,340	42.2	1,888
51	Pontiac Aztek†	19,995	41.4	1,901
52	Chrysler Town & Country†	23,675	41.1	2,036
53	Land Rover Freelander†	24,975	41.0	2,088
54	Chevrolet Trailblazer EXT-I6	30,785	41.0	2,268
55	Dodge Durango†	24,875	40.9	2,073
56	Dodge Grand Caravan†	21,785	40.6	1,955
57	Lincoln Blackwood	51,785	40.6	3,020
58	Chevrolet Astro†	21,013	39.7	1,907
59	GMC Safari†	21,013	39.7	1,907
60	Kia Sportage-4 Cyl.	14,645	39.2	1,646
61	Isuzu Axiom	26,535	39.1	2,096
62	Ford Windstar	20,385	38.1	1,849
63	Mercury Mountaineer†	28,690	37.4	2,124
64	Land Rover Discovery†	33,350	37.4	2,270
65	Dodge Caravan†	16,355	37.1	1,685
66	Chevrolet Venture†	21,280	36.6	1,850
67	Lincoln Navigator	44,115	36.1	2,583
68	Kia Sedona†	18,995	35.8	1,595
69	Oldsmobile Bravada†	31,635	35.1	2,155
70	Mercedes-Benz M Class-V8†	65,900	34.7	3,283
71	Pontiac Montana†	24,235	34.5	1,906
72	Isuzu Trooper	27,470	34.3	2,009
73	Oldsmobile Silhouette†	26,805	32.2	1,931
74	Land Rover Range Rover	68,000	27.8	2,898

* *Consumer Reports* "reliable used cars."   † *Consumer Reports* "used cars to avoid."

RANKING OF 2003 USED SPORT UTILITY VEHICLES AND SMALL VANS BY NADA RETAIL VALUE IN SEPTEMBER 2007 AS A PERCENTAGE OF ORIGINAL MANUFACTURER'S SUGGESTED RETAIL VALUE

Rank	Model	Original M.S.R.P.	Retail Value as Percent of M.S.R.P.	Retail Value minus Trade-In
1	Jeep Wrangler	$15,665	95.4	$2,324
2	Toyota RAV4*	16,525	92.0	2,375
3	Volkswagen Eurovan†	26,200	82.3	2,981
4	Honda Element*	16,100	81.8	2,188
5	Honda CR-V*	18,900	77.6	2,325
6	Infiniti FX*	34,200	75.4	3,313
7	Porsche Cayenne	55,900	74.0	4,956
8	Toyota 4Runner*	27,205	73.3	2,879
9	Jeep Liberty*	17,235	72.6	2,271
10	Nissan Xterra V6*	20,399	71.5	2,473
11	Nissan Murano	28,199	71.3	2,710
12	BMW X5-I6	39,500	70.5	3,436
13	Toyota Sequoia	31,625	69.3	3,044
14	Lexus GX470*	44,925	68.4	3,655
15	Toyota Highlander*	23,880	66.3	2,416
16	Volvo XC90†	33,350	65.5	3,069
17	Honda Pilot*	26,900	65.1	2,498
18	Hummer H2†	48,065	64.3	3,694
19	Isuzu Rodeo Sport	13,999	63.8	1,965
20	Lexus RX300*	35,125	63.6	3,098
21	Nissan Xterra-4 Cyl.*	17,999	63.2	2,183
22	Honda Odyssey*	24,400	63.0	2,544
23	Mitsubishi Outlander*	17,997	63.0	2,172
24	Hyundai Santa Fe*	17,399	62.9	2,139
25	Ford Escape	18,800	62.6	2,210
26	Acura MDX*	35,700	61.6	3,074
27	Ford Excursion	35,616	61.5	3,011
28	Saturn Vue	16,900	61.4	2,093
29	Kia Sorento†	19,500	60.0	2,201
30	Lexus LX470*	63,125	59.6	4,523
31	Mazda Tribute V6	21,585	59.3	2,293
32	Toyota Sienna*	23,905	59.3	2,436
33	Ford Explorer†	21,505	59.1	2,303
34	Toyota Land Cruiser*	53,405	59.0	3,773
35	Suzuki XL-7	19,599	58.7	2,184
36	Nissan Pathfinder	26,799	58.1	2,553
37	Mercedes-benz M Class†	36,600	57.6	2,998
38	Chevrolet Tahoe	33,506	55.8	2,783
39	Suzuki Grand Vitara	18,599	55.7	2,090
40	Ford Expedition†	30,555	54.9	2,633
41	Chevrolet Trailblazer†	25,950	54.7	2,435
42	GMC Yukon	34,272	54.5	2,783
43	Mitsubishi Montero	22,907	54.0	2,268
44	BMW X5	66,800	53.7	4,310
45	Cadillac Escalade	49,710	53.6	3,366

RANKING OF 2003 USED SPORT UTILITY VEHICLES AND SMALL VANS
(Continued)

Rank	Model	Original M.S.R.P.	Retail Value as Percent of M.S.R.P.	Retail Value minus Trade-In
46	Mazda Tribute-4 Cyl.	$18,200	53.6	2,045
47	Mazda MPV	21,285	53.5	2,178
48	Chevrolet Suburban†	36,240	53.2	2,826
49	GMC Envoy†	27,875	53.2	2,497
50	Infiniti QX4*	34,750	52.7	2,726
51	Chevrolet Tracker	16,240	52.5	1,926
52	Suzuki Vitara	15,599	52.4	1,894
53	Chevrolet SSR	41,370	51.6	3,035
54	Jeep Grand Cherokee†	28,935	51.3	2,493
55	Jeep Grand Cherokee†	26,045	51.3	2,358
56	Isuzu Ascender	28,649	51.2	2,489
57	Isuzu Axiom	24,345	50.9	2,268
58	GMC Denali	44,250	50.6	3,098
59	Land Rover Range Rover	69,330	50.5	4,263
60	Land Rover Discovery†	34,350	49.9	2,654
61	Chevrolet Blazer†	20,080	49.8	2,062
62	Chrysler Town & Country†	23,900	49.7	2,225
63	Land Rover Freelander	24,975	49.7	2,259
64	Mercury Mountaineer†	29,180	49.4	2,458
65	Dodge Grand Caravan†	21,325	49.1	2,101
66	Buick Rendezvous†	25,120	48.1	2,239
67	Chevrolet Trailblazer EXT V8†	31,135	48.1	2,517
68	Lincoln Navigator†	48,035	48.1	3,145
69	Lincoln Aviator†	39,255	47.4	2,751
70	Dodge Durango	26,130	47.1	2,258
71	Pontiac Aztek†	20,295	47.0	2,026
72	Ford Windstar	20,705	45.2	1,992
73	Chevrolet Astro†	21,272	45.1	2,028
74	GMC Safari†	21,272	45.1	2,028
75	Chevrolet Venture	21,363	43.1	1,984
76	Kia Sedona†	19,370	43.0	1,738
77	Chrysler Voyager†	20,125	43.0	1,938
78	Dodge Caravan†	19,805	42.2	1,911
79	Pontiac Montana	24,164	41.5	2,063
80	Oldsmobile Bravada†	32,570	41.1	2,355
81	Mercedes-benz M Class V8	65,900	40.2	3,655
82	Oldsmobile Silhouette	27,830	40.0	2,153

* *Consumer Reports* "reliable used cars."   † *Consumer Reports* "used cars to avoid."

RANKING OF 2004 USED SPORT UTILITY VEHICLES AND SMALL VANS
BY NADA RETAIL VALUE IN SEPTEMBER 2007 AS A PERCENTAGE OF ORIGINAL MANUFACTURER'S SUGGESTED RETAIL VALUE

Rank	Model	Original M.S.R.P.	Retail Value as Percent of M.S.R.P.	Retail Value minus Trade-In
1	Jeep Wrangler	$16,270	102.5	$2,440
2	Porsche Cayenne†	42,900	98.9	4,958
3	BMW X5-I6†	40,300	93.5	4,284
4	Toyota RAV4*	18,350	93.0	2,473
5	Honda Element*	17,100	87.7	2,351
6	Honda CR-V*	19,000	85.7	2,435
7	Nissan Xterra V6	19,400	84.8	2,615
8	BMW X3†	30,300	84.1	3,296
9	Lexus RX330*	35,025	83.3	3,513
10	Infiniti FX*	34,350	83.1	3,502
11	Toyota 4Runner*	27,170	81.8	3,078
12	Saturn Vue	16,775	80.8	2,380
13	Toyota Sienna	22,955	80.0	2,570
14	Toyota Sequoia*	31,625	79.8	3,276
15	Jeep Liberty*	18,010	78.6	2,437
16	Lexus GX470*	45,075	78.3	3,985
17	Volkswagen Touareg V10†	57,800	77.4	4,720
18	Nissan Murano	28,200	77.4	2,824
19	Honda Pilot*	27,100	74.9	2,725
20	Mitsubishi Outlander*	17,702	73.9	2,317
21	Toyota Highlander*	24,080	73.8	2,516
22	Honda Odyssey*	24,490	73.5	2,710
23	Ford Escape	18,710	73.4	2,393
24	Hyundai Santa Fe*	17,999	73.0	2,346
25	Volvo XC90†	34,440	72.8	3,271
26	Acura MDX*	36,400	72.6	3,355
27	Nissan Xterra-4 Cyl.	18,000	71.9	2,285
28	Hummer H2	49,180	71.0	3,964
29	Suzuki Grand Vitara†	17,499	70.9	2,270
30	Suzuki XL-7†	19,499	70.9	2,404
31	Nissan Armada†	33,300	69.6	3,151
32	Kia Sorento	18,995	69.6	2,334
33	Ford Excursion†	36,435	69.1	3,267
34	Volkswagen Touareg V6†	34,900	69.0	3,208
35	Mercedes-Benz M Class	38,020	67.9	3,316
36	Toyota Land Cruiser*	54,225	67.6	4,223
37	Mazda Tribute V6	21,950	67.5	2,505
38	Isuzu Rodeo	19,799	67.5	2,351
39	Nissan Quest†	24,240	67.4	2,607
40	Lexus LX470*	64,175	67.2	4,885
41	Volkswagen Touareg V8†	40,700	66.7	3,398
42	Infiniti QX56†	50,500	66.6	3,888
43	Nissan Pathfinder*	26,900	66.5	2,702
44	Chevrolet Tahoe	34,200	65.0	3,081
45	Chrysler Town & Country†	22,855	64.6	2,468

RANKING OF 2004 USED SPORT UTILITY VEHICLES AND SMALL VANS
(Continued)

Rank	Model	Original M.S.R.P.	Retail Value as Percent of M.S.R.P.	Retail Value minus Trade-In
46	Suzuki Vitara	$16,299	64.2	2,105
47	GMC Yukon	34,910	63.6	3,081
48	Land Rover Freelander	25,330	63.5	2,594
49	GMC Denali	41,180	63.3	3,331
50	Dodge Durango	25,920	62.4	2,588
51	Land Rover Discovery†	34,330	62.3	3,001
52	Isuzu Ascender 5 Passenger I6	25,699	62.3	2,586
53	Chevrolet Suburban	37,050	61.9	3,138
54	Isuzu Axiom	24,849	60.7	2,521
55	Cadillac Escalade†	51,980	60.7	3,729
56	Ford Explorer†	26,285	60.1	2,543
57	Mazda MPV	23,260	59.7	2,403
58	Mitsubishi Montero	23,797	59.3	2,426
59	Chevrolet SSR	41,370	58.7	3,223
60	Mazda Tribute-4 Cyl.	18,565	58.4	2,134
61	Mitsubishi Endeavor	25,002	58.2	2,465
62	Mercury Mountaineer†	29,350	57.9	2,651
63	Ford Expedition†	31,940	57.8	2,778
64	Jeep Grand Cherokee†	27,110	57.6	2,555
65	Land Rover Range Rover	71,585	57.6	4,713
66	Cadillac SRX†	37,995	56.8	3,029
67	Chevrolet Blazer†	20,745	56.6	2,207
68	Chevrolet Tracker	19,780	56.5	2,159
69	Buick Rendezvous*	25,895	56.5	2,469
70	Dodge Grand Caravan†	22,790	56.5	2,327
71	GMC Envoy XL†	32,445	56.3	2,726
72	Chevrolet Trailblazer	27,145	56.1	2,531
73	Lincoln Navigator†	48,485	55.6	3,386
74	Chrysler Pacifica†	28,845	55.0	2,413
75	Isuzu Ascender 7 Passenger V8	33,496	54.9	2,734
76	Lincoln Aviator†	39,710	53.5	3,015
77	Ford Freestar	21,385	53.5	2,187
78	Pontiac Aztek	20,995	52.6	2,154
79	Chevrolet Astro†	22,260	51.8	2,184
80	GMC Safari†	22,260	51.8	2,184
81	Kia Sedona†	19,975	51.5	1,891
82	Pontiac Montana	23,165	50.9	2,213
83	Mercury Monterey†	29,310	49.2	2,456
84	Chevrolet Venture	21,315	49.1	2,100
85	Dodge Caravan†	21,130	48.2	2,077
86	Buick Rainier†	35,295	48.1	2,646
87	Oldsmobile Bravada	33,645	48.0	2,596
88	Oldsmobile Silhouette	28,110	46.9	2,336

* *Consumer Reports* "reliable used cars." † *Consumer Reports* "used cars to avoid."

RANKING OF 2005 USED SPORT UTILITY VEHICLES AND SMALL VANS
BY NADA RETAIL VALUE IN SEPTEMBER 2007 AS A PERCENTAGE
OF ORIGINAL MANUFACTURER'S SUGGESTED RETAIL VALUE

Rank	Model	Original M.S.R.P.	Retail Value as Percent of M.S.R.P.	Retail Value minus Trade-In
1	Porsche Cayenne†	$41,100	116.7	$5,338
2	Jeep Wrangler†	17,900	105.0	2,601
3	BMW X5†	41,700	102.9	4,654
4	Toyota RAV4*	18,550	101.3	2,758
5	Honda Odyssey	24,995	98.8	3,244
6	Honda Element*	17,450	96.8	2,466
7	Honda CR-V*	19,995	95.2	2,631
8	BMW X3	30,300	94.0	3,475
9	Nissan Xterra	20,800	93.0	2,834
10	Kia Sportage†	15,900	92.9	2,505
11	Nissan Pathfinder	24,650	92.6	3,131
12	Lexus RX330*	35,775	91.9	3,844
13	Infiniti FX*	34,750	91.8	3,766
14	Toyota Sequoia*	32,470	91.7	3,587
15	Saturn Vue	17,055	89.6	2,518
16	Toyota 4Runner*	27,495	89.4	3,238
17	Toyota Sienna*	23,225	89.0	2,715
18	Lexus GX470*	45,775	88.8	4,433
19	Volvo XC90†	34,840	86.8	3,638
20	Nissan Murano*	26,850	86.7	2,898
21	Ford Escape	19,405	86.2	2,635
22	Mitsubishi Outlander	17,799	86.0	2,523
23	Honda Pilot*	27,350	85.2	2,903
24	Jeep Liberty†	19,190	85.2	2,607
25	Acura MDX*	36,700	83.2	3,665
26	Kia Sorento	18,995	82.3	2,558
27	Toyota Highlander*	24,080	82.0	2,666
28	Toyota Land Cruiser*	55,025	80.7	4,703
29	Chrysler Town & Country†	20,330	79.5	2,594
30	Mercedes-Benz M Class	37,950	79.5	3,630
31	Ford Excursion†	37,015	79.3	3,596
32	Hummer H2†	50,950	78.8	4,408
33	Infiniti QX56†	47,750	78.4	4,245
34	Nissan Armada†	33,600	77.9	3,338
35	Nissan Quest†	23,350	77.8	2,752
36	Hyundai Tucson	17,499	77.6	2,383
37	Suzuki Grand Vitara	18,399	77.1	2,429
38	Land Rover LR3†	41,285	76.7	4,080
39	Mazda Tribute	19,320	76.1	2,493
40	Suzuki XL-7	20,399	75.7	2,547
41	Lexus LX470*	64,775	74.8	5,235
42	GMC Denali	41,735	74.5	3,702
43	Chevrolet Tahoe	35,000	73.9	3,316
44	Chevrolet Equinox†	20,995	73.3	2,541
45	Hyundai Santa Fe*	21,649	73.3	2,578

RANKING OF 2005 USED SPORT UTILITY VEHICLES AND SMALL VANS
(Continued)

Rank	Model	Original M.S.R.P.	Retail Value as Percent of M.S.R.P.	Retail Value minus Trade-In
46	GMC Yukon	$35,460	72.9	3,316
47	Jeep Grand Cherokee V8†	28,430	72.4	2,944
48	Mercury Mariner	21,405	71.8	2,548
49	Dodge Grand Caravan†	20,015	71.4	2,433
50	Chrysler Pacifica†	24,315	71.1	2,491
51	Ford Expedition†	32,570	70.9	3,108
52	Volkswagen Touareg V6†	37,140	70.8	3,353
53	Chevrolet Suburban	37,850	69.7	3,348
54	Saab 9-7X	38,270	68.8	3,353
55	Ford Freestyle†	24,945	68.6	2,479
56	Ford Explorer	26,770	68.5	2,779
57	Mazda MPV*	22,105	68.2	2,518
58	Land Rover Freelander	26,830	68.2	2,728
59	Isuzu Ascender 5 Passenger I6	25,959	68.2	2,691
60	Chevrolet SSR	42,430	68.1	3,500
61	Land Rover Range Rover	73,085	68.1	5,308
62	Cadillac Escalade†	52,635	68.0	4,082
63	Mitsubishi Endeavor†	25,399	67.8	2,680
64	Saturn RELAY†	23,770	67.8	2,594
65	Mitsubishi Montero	35,799	67.7	3,210
66	Dodge Durango	26,735	67.3	2,727
67	Chevrolet Uplander†	20,700	67.3	2,402
68	Mercury Mountaineer	29,525	66.6	2,875
69	Jeep Grand Cherokee V6†	26,130	65.6	2,656
70	Dodge Caravan†	18,330	65.5	2,235
71	Cadillac SRX†	38,340	65.4	3,269
72	Buick Rendezvous*	26,455	65.1	2,680
73	Chevrolet Blazer†	21,055	63.8	2,356
74	Lincoln Navigator†	49,640	63.8	3,749
75	Pontiac Montana SV6	24,520	62.8	2,549
76	GMC Envoy	29,550	62.8	2,772
77	Kia Sedona†	20,200	62.6	2,134
78	Lincoln Aviator†	40,460	62.4	3,281
79	Chevrolet Trailblazer	27,520	61.9	2,651
80	Chevrolet Astro†	22,695	61.4	2,397
81	GMC Safari†	22,695	61.4	2,397
82	Isuzu Ascender 7 Passenger V8	33,596	61.3	2,963
83	Ford Freestar	21,610	60.4	2,320
84	Buick Terraza†	28,110	60.3	2,645
85	Pontiac Aztek	21,275	60.3	2,299
86	Pontiac Montana†	26,040	55.1	2,450
87	Buick Rainier	34,940	54.8	2,784
88	Mercury Monterey	29,310	54.6	2,589
89	Chevrolet Venture	23,165	53.3	2,250

* *Consumer Reports* "reliable used cars."   † *Consumer Reports* "used cars to avoid."

RANKING OF 2006 USED SPORT UTILITY VEHICLES AND SMALL VANS
BY NADA RETAIL VALUE IN SEPTEMBER 2007 AS A PERCENTAGE OF ORIGINAL MANUFACTURER'S SUGGESTED RETAIL VALUE

Rank	Model	Original M.S.R.P.	Retail Value as Percent of M.S.R.P.	Retail Value minus Trade-In
1	Porsche Cayenne	$42,200	151.2	$6,441
2	BMW X5†	42,500	118.0	5,100
3	Jeep Wrangler†	18,070	114.4	2,720
4	Land Rover Range Rover†	56,085	113.5	6,229
5	Honda Odyssey	25,345	113.3	3,517
6	Honda Element*	17,750	109.0	2,638
7	Toyota RAV4*	20,300	108.0	2,828
8	Toyota Highlander V6*	25,590	106.8	3,196
9	Mercedes-Benz M Class†	39,750	106.7	4,559
10	Toyota Sequoia*	32,820	106.2	3,998
11	Kia Sportage-4 Cyl.†	15,900	105.7	2,639
12	Nissan Xterra*	19,950	104.7	2,986
13	Saturn Vue	17,390	102.9	2,729
14	Lexus RX330*	36,370	102.5	4,246
15	Honda CR-V*	20,395	102.5	2,755
16	Nissan Pathfinder	25,250	102.0	3,309
17	Toyota 4Runner*	27,635	101.5	3,469
18	Toyota Sienna*	23,625	101.3	2,950
19	Lexus GX470*	46,535	99.7	4,808
20	Volvo XC90†	35,640	99.4	4,039
21	Honda Pilot*	26,995	99.2	3,142
22	Hummer H3†	28,935	99.1	3,484
23	Ford Escape	19,380	98.2	2,807
24	Jeep Grand Cherokee V8†	27,885	97.0	3,411
25	Acura MDX*	37,125	97.0	4,121
26	Infiniti FX	37,800	96.9	4,127
27	Kia Sportage V6†	19,100	96.3	2,734
28	BMW X3†	36,800	95.7	3,980
29	Lexus RX400h*	44,660	92.6	4,504
30	Mercury Mariner-4 Cyl.	21,380	92.4	2,858
31	Jeep Commander V8†	28,010	92.0	3,307
32	Toyota Highlander-4 Cyl.*	24,530	91.7	2,861
33	Nissan Murano	27,450	91.7	3,032
34	Mitsubishi Outlander	18,499	91.5	2,648
35	Kia Sorento	18,995	91.2	2,669
36	Chrysler Town & Country	21,020	91.0	2,833
37	Toyota Land Cruiser	55,815	89.6	5,070
38	Mercedes-Benz R Class†	48,000	89.3	4,584
39	Suzuki Grand Vitara†	18,999	89.2	2,647
40	Jeep Liberty†	20,970	88.1	2,769
41	Hyundai Tucson	17,495	87.8	2,548
42	Infiniti QX56†	49,550	87.3	4,639
43	Nissan Quest†	24,000	86.8	2,943
44	GMC Denali	41,735	86.4	4,133
45	Land Rover LR3†	38,285	86.2	4,155

RANKING OF 2006 USED SPORT UTILITY VEHICLES AND SMALL VANS
(Continued)

Rank	Model	Original M.S.R.P.	Retail Value as Percent of M.S.R.P.	Retail Value minus Trade-In
46	Toyota Highlander Hybrid*	$36,160	86.1	3,473
47	Nissan Armada†	34,500	85.6	3,584
48	Chevrolet TrailBlazer V8	27,850	85.5	3,164
49	Ford Explorer†	26,530	85.3	3,088
50	Ford Escape Hybrid†	27,713	85.3	3,178
51	Hummer H2	52,980	84.3	4,714
52	Lexus LX470*	66,995	84.1	5,725
53	Mercury Mariner V6	23,285	83.6	2,838
54	Chevrolet Tahoe†	35,915	83.1	3,613
55	Volkswagen Touareg V6†	37,320	82.7	3,705
56	GMC Yukon†	34,805	82.4	3,526
57	Pontiac Torrent	22,400	82.1	2,734
58	Chrysler Pacifica	25,165	81.9	2,724
59	Dodge Grand Caravan	20,615	81.6	2,633
60	Hyundai Santa Fe*	21,695	81.4	2,689
61	Ford Expedition†	32,660	81.3	3,378
62	Subaru B9 Tribeca*	30,695	81.2	3,258
63	Chevrolet Equinox	21,755	81.1	2,689
64	Ford Freestar†	19,650	81.0	2,548
65	Mazda Tribute	20,115	80.8	2,601
66	Saab 9-7X	38,520	80.3	3,720
67	Chevrolet Suburban†	38,765	80.2	3,706
68	Mitsubishi Montero	36,159	79.4	3,485
69	Suzuki XL-7	21,999	79.1	2,676
70	Mercury Mountaineer†	29,150	77.7	3,118
71	Dodge Caravan	18,380	77.5	2,435
72	Mazda MPV	22,115	76.9	2,650
73	Mitsubishi Endeavor	26,599	76.8	2,918
74	Cadillac Escalade	53,335	76.8	4,469
75	Isuzu Ascender 5 Passenger I6	25,959	76.7	2,891
76	Cadillac SRX†	39,275	76.5	3,624
77	Ford Freestyle	25,105	76.5	2,627
78	Saturn RELAY†	23,970	76.1	2,726
79	Kia Sedona	22,995	74.9	2,488
80	Lincoln Navigator†	50,500	74.0	4,198
81	Chevrolet Uplander†	20,900	73.6	2,529
82	Dodge Durango†	28,200	73.4	2,964
83	Jeep Commander V6†	27,290	72.9	2,888
84	GMC Envoy	28,590	72.8	2,974
85	Chevrolet Trailblazer I6	26,700	71.6	2,809
86	Jeep Grand Cherokee V6†	27,165	70.7	2,799
87	Buick Rendezvous*	26,595	70.7	2,791
88	Isuzu Ascender 7 Passenger V8	33,337	69.1	3,141
89	Pontiac Montana SV6†	24,840	68.6	2,650
90	Buick Terraza†	27,790	67.0	2,746

RANKING OF 2006 USED SPORT UTILITY VEHICLES AND SMALL VANS
(Continued)

Rank	Model	Original M.S.R.P.	Retail Value as Percent of M.S.R.P.	Retail Value minus Trade-In
91	Buick Rainier	$33,075	65.8	3,064
92	Mercury Monterey†	28,595	64.5	2,735

* *Consumer Reports* "reliable used cars." † *Consumer Reports* "used cars to avoid."

RANKING OF 2002 USED LIGHT PICKUPS
BY NADA RETAIL VALUE IN SEPTEMBER 2007 AS A PERCENTAGE OF ORIGINAL MANUFACTURER'S SUGGESTED RETAIL VALUE

Rank	Model	Original M.S.R.P.	Retail Value as Percent of M.S.R.P.	Retail Value minus Trade-In
1	Toyota Tacoma-4 Cyl.*	$11,900	100.5	$2,173
2	Toyota Tacoma Double Cab V6*	18,970	91.3	2,540
3	Toyota Tacoma V6*	18,060	83.6	2,390
4	Nissan Frontier King Cab V6*	15,999	80.1	2,305
5	Nissan Frontier Crew Cab*	18,199	78.7	2,448
6	Toyota Tacoma Double Cab-4 Cyl.*	18,110	78.5	2,325
7	Toyota Tundra V6*	15,605	76.5	2,227
8	Nissan Frontier King Cab-4 Cyl.*	12,799	74.5	2,023
9	Ford Ranger	12,110	72.8	1,949
10	Chevrolet Silverado 1500*	17,168	69.6	2,216
11	Ford F150 Pickup*	18,049	69.2	2,271
12	Chevrolet S10 Pickup†	13,625	68.6	1,991
13	GMC Sonoma†	13,639	68.5	1,991
14	Toyota Tundra V8*	22,975	64.3	2,471
15	Dodge Ram 1500†	16,955	64.3	2,138
16	GMC Sierra 1500*	18,803	63.5	2,216
17	Dodge Dakota†	14,610	62.6	1,981
18	Mazda B3000	15,285	61.1	1,995
19	Ford F150 Supercrew*	26,915	59.0	2,577
20	Ford Explorer Sport Trac	22,010	56.7	2,258
21	Mazda B2300	12,655	56.4	1,787
22	Mazda B4000	19,500	55.6	2,138
23	Chevrolet Avalanche†	30,245	52.1	2,572
24	Chevrolet Silverado 1500 HD	28,605	51.7	2,495
25	GMC Sierra 1500 HD	29,323	50.4	2,495

* *Consumer Reports* "reliable used cars."   † *Consumer Reports* "used cars to avoid."

RANKING OF 2003 USED LIGHT PICKUPS
BY NADA RETAIL VALUE IN SEPTEMBER 2007 AS A PERCENTAGE OF ORIGINAL MANUFACTURER'S SUGGESTED RETAIL VALUE

Rank	Model	Original M.S.R.P.	Retail Value as Percent of M.S.R.P.	Retail Value minus Trade-In
1	Toyota Tacoma-4 Cyl.*	$12,100	107.5	$2,168
2	Toyota Tacoma V6*	17,555	98.9	2,488
3	Toyota Tacoma Double Cab V6*	19,170	98.4	2,595
4	Nissan Frontier King Cab V6*	16,169	90.5	2,478
5	Nissan Frontier Crew Cab*	18,439	87.9	2,592
6	Toyota Tundra V6*	15,955	86.9	2,395
7	Toyota Tacoma Double Cab-4 Cyl.*	18,310	84.6	2,400
8	Nissan Frontier King Cab-4 Cyl.*	12,989	82.4	2,129
9	Chevrolet Silverado 1500	18,191	82.1	2,494
10	Ford Ranger*	13,010	75.9	2,050
11	Ford F150*	18,715	75.2	2,407
12	Chevrolet S10 Pickup†	14,161	74.3	2,109
13	GMC Sonoma†	14,175	74.2	2,109
14	GMC Sierra 1500	18,603	72.7	2,371
15	Toyota Tundra V8*	23,325	72.6	2,646
16	Dodge Ram 1500	17,920	68.7	2,259
17	Ford Explorer Sport Trac*	22,355	65.2	2,474
18	Ford F150 Supercrew*	27,580	64.7	2,730
19	Dodge Dakota	16,090	63.8	2,079
20	Mazda B4000*	19,800	61.1	2,229
21	Mazda B2300*	13,345	60.4	1,872
22	Mazda B3000*	16,190	60.3	2,040
23	Chevrolet Avalanche†	31,394	59.2	2,751
24	Chevrolet Silverado 1500 HD†	29,677	56.0	2,625
25	GMC Sierra 1500 HD†	30,220	55.0	2,625

* *Consumer Reports* "reliable used cars."   † *Consumer Reports* "used cars to avoid."

RANKING OF 2004 USED LIGHT PICKUPS
BY NADA RETAIL VALUE IN SEPTEMBER 2007 AS A PERCENTAGE OF ORIGINAL MANUFACTURER'S SUGGESTED RETAIL VALUE

Rank	Model	Original M.S.R.P.	Retail Value as Percent of M.S.R.P.	Retail Value minus Trade-In
1	Toyota Tacoma-4 Cyl.*	$12,260	116.5	$2,278
2	Toyota Tacoma Double Cab V6*	19,350	106.4	2,734
3	Toyota Tacoma V6*	17,735	106.3	2,600
4	Nissan Frontier King Cab V6*	16,490	99.7	2,603
5	Toyota Tundra V6*	15,955	98.8	2,528
6	Dodge Ram 1500	18,970	96.0	2,733
7	Nissan Frontier Crew Cab*	18,820	94.0	2,700
8	Toyota Tacoma Double Cab-4 Cyl.*	18,490	92.1	2,475
9	Nissan Frontier King Cab-4 Cyl.*	13,290	89.5	2,218
10	Chevrolet Silverado 1500†	19,995	85.9	2,667
11	Toyota Tundra Double Cab V8*	25,645	85.6	3,046
12	Toyota Tundra V8*	23,445	84.3	2,873
13	GMC Canyon†	14,915	82.3	2,265
14	Ford Ranger*	13,765	80.9	2,155
15	Ford F150 Heritage*	19,125	80.0	2,509
16	Chevrolet Colorado†	15,565	79.5	2,273
17	GMC Sierra 1500†	20,652	78.8	2,590
18	Nissan Titan†	22,400	77.4	2,684
19	Ford Explorer Sport Trac	23,045	74.3	2,656
20	Ford F150†	21,215	72.1	2,516
21	Ford F150 Supercrew	29,020	70.3	2,942
22	Dodge Dakota†	16,940	69.1	2,208
23	Chevrolet Avalanche†	32,285	67.7	3,068
24	Chevrolet S10†	24,460	67.1	2,613
25	GMC Sonoma†	24,760	66.3	2,613
26	Mazda B4000*	20,230	66.0	2,355
27	Mazda B2300*	14,220	63.9	1,972
28	Mazda B3000*	17,295	63.5	2,147

* *Consumer Reports* "reliable used cars."   † *Consumer Reports* "used cars to avoid."

RANKING OF 2005 USED LIGHT PICKUPS
BY NADA RETAIL VALUE IN SEPTEMBER 2007 AS A PERCENTAGE OF ORIGINAL MANUFACTURER'S SUGGESTED RETAIL VALUE

Rank	Model	Original M.S.R.P.	Retail Value as Percent of M.S.R.P.	Retail Value minus Trade-In
1	Toyota Tacoma-4 Cyl.*	$13,415	116.1	$2,369
2	Dodge Ram 1500	20,180	113.9	3,105
3	Toyota Tundra V8*	18,430	111.8	2,952
4	Toyota Tacoma V6*	19,070	104.0	2,688
5	Nissan Frontier Crew Cab	20,550	100.6	2,747
6	Nissan Frontier King Cab V6	18,400	100.6	2,583
7	Toyota Tacoma Double Cab V6*	21,675	99.0	2,800
8	Toyota Tundra V6*	15,955	98.4	2,515
9	Toyota Tundra Double Cab V8*	26,120	94.8	3,248
10	Chevrolet Silverado 1500	20,610	92.7	2,819
11	Nissan Frontier King Cab-4 Cyl.	15,500	92.4	2,288
12	Chevrolet Colorado†	15,695	92.3	2,457
13	GMC Canyon†	16,025	87.6	2,420
14	Nissan Titan†	22,650	87.4	2,881
15	GMC Sierra 1500	21,270	86.7	2,768
16	Ford F150	19,610	85.5	2,651
17	Ford Ranger*	14,635	84.9	2,275
18	Ford Explorer Sport Trac*	23,710	83.8	2,886
19	Dodge Dakota†	18,565	81.4	2,505
20	Ford F150 Supercrew†	29,390	77.3	3,125
21	Chevrolet Avalanche*	33,320	75.1	3,272
22	Mazda B4000*	21,600	73.4	2,581
23	Chevrolet Silverado 1500 HD†	31,495	68.3	3,050
24	GMC Sierra 1500 HD†	31,995	67.2	3,050
25	Mazda B3000*	18,860	65.4	2,271
26	Mazda B2300*	15,315	62.9	2,031

* *Consumer Reports* "reliable used cars." † *Consumer Reports* "used cars to avoid."

RANKING OF 2006 USED LIGHT PICKUPS
BY NADA RETAIL VALUE IN SEPTEMBER 2007 AS A PERCENTAGE OF ORIGINAL MANUFACTURER'S SUGGESTED RETAIL VALUE

Rank	Model	Original M.S.R.P.	Retail Value as Percent of M.S.R.P.	Retail Value minus Trade-In
1	Toyota Tacoma-4 Cyl.*	$13,780	126.4	$2,510
2	Dodge Ram 1500	20,800	124.1	3,313
3	Toyota Tundra V8	18,630	122.4	3,100
4	Toyota Tacoma V6*	19,435	113.0	2,832
5	Toyota Tundra V6*	16,155	110.0	2,758
6	Toyota Tacoma Double Cab*	22,040	108.7	2,968
7	Nissan Frontier Crew Cab*	20,850	108.6	2,867
8	Nissan Frontier King Cab V6†	19,000	106.8	2,699
9	Toyota Tundra Double Cab*	26,620	102.5	3,401
10	Chevrolet Colorado	15,330	102.3	2,543
11	Chevrolet Silverado 1500	21,375	102.1	3,045
12	Nissan Frontier King Cab-4 Cyl.*	15,800	100.3	2,410
13	GMC Canyon	15,660	100.1	2,541
14	Ford Ranger	14,450	99.4	2,450
15	Ford F150†	18,790	98.4	2,777
16	Nissan Titan*	23,250	97.3	3,097
17	GMC Sierra 1500	21,610	94.3	2,949
18	Ford F150 Supercab†	23,940	91.9	3,053
19	Honda Ridgeline	27,700	90.9	3,275
20	Chevrolet SSR	39,340	86.5	3,910
21	Dodge Dakota†	20,010	85.6	2,658
22	Chevrolet Avalanche*	34,010	83.8	3,474
23	Isuzu i-280	16,989	83.8	2,436
24	Ford F150 Supercrew†	30,015	83.8	3,275
25	Mitsubishi Raider	23,680	81.9	2,863
26	Mazda B4000*	21,895	81.3	2,694
27	Lincoln Mark LT	38,680	79.4	3,664
28	GMC Sierra 1500 HD†	32,480	77.0	3,265
29	Mazda B3000	18,890	75.4	2,433
30	Chevrolet Silverado 1500 HD†	31,980	75.1	3,200
31	Isuzu i-350	27,358	74.1	2,909
32	Mazda B2300	15,340	73.6	2,168

* *Consumer Reports* "reliable used cars."   † *Consumer Reports* "used cars to avoid."

III.

THE AUTOMOBILE PRICE OUTLOOK

THERE are two major components to the price you pay when you buy a car. One is the purchase price, and the other, for those who buy on credit, is the cost of the loan. The cost of a loan depends, in turn, on the three key variables: the amount you borrow, the interest rate you are charged, and the length of the loan. Other factors, of course, affect the ultimate cost of *owning* a car (such as outlays for fuel, repairs, maintenance, and insurance, as well as the rate at which the vehicle's resale value decreases). But these are not part of the terms of *acquiring* a car. Moreover, in contrast to many of the costs of ownership, the purchase price and the terms of the loan are **negotiable**.

It is important to become informed about the major factors that may affect your ability to negotiate a favorable purchase price and favorable terms on a loan. For example, if auto manufacturers are likely to raise prices or cut back on their financial incentives, it may be to your advantage to buy a car now rather than delay. Similarly, if interest rates are likely to increase in the near future, you may be better off buying now rather than later.

Many factors affect the trend of car prices. In recent years, price increases have been modest, reflecting intensive competition among automobile manufacturers. Table 2a shows the manufacturers' suggested retail prices (the "sticker prices") for the cars that were "recommended" by *Consumer Reports* both last year and this year. As can be seen, their M.S.R.P.s changed by anywhere from -4.5 to 2.1 percent, with most models showing no change. Table 2b shows similar information for "recommended" trucks, minivans, and sport utility vehicles (SUVs), with the change in prices ranging from 0.0 to 6.6 percent.

A portion of the increase in sticker price often reflects improvements to the vehicles. In other words, car makers may be asking more, but they are offering you "more car" for your money. Features that were once optional, such as anti-lock brakes, may become standard. They may offer new features that were previously available only on luxury cars, if at all—for example, side curtain air bags or heated seats. The general quality of cars has improved greatly over the years. Today's cars require less maintenance and fewer repairs than they used to, and they also have better warranties. To

Table 2a
2006 vs. 2007 M.S.R.P. FOR SELECTED MODELS*

Model	2006 M.S.R.P.	2007 M.S.R.P.	Percent Change
Chrysler PT Cruiser Ltd (turbo)	$23,485	$23,485	0.0
Chevrolet Malibu Maxx LT (V6)	23,225	23,225	0.0
Ford Focus ZX4 SES	19,080	19,080	0.0
Ford Focus ZX5 S	18,750	18,750	0.0
Honda Accord EX	23,515	23,515	0.0
Honda Civic EX	19,610	19,610	0.0
Honda Civic Hybrid	22,400	22,400	0.0
Mazda 3i	18,190	18,190	0.0
Mazda 6i (4-cyl)	21,930	21,930	0.0
Mitsubishi Galant ES (4-cyl)	20,944	20,944	0.0
Scion xB	14,995	14,995	0.0
Scion xB (manual)	14,245	14,245	0.0
Scion tC	17,115	17,115	0.0
Pontiac Vibe (FWD)	19,960	19,960	0.0
Subaru Impreza 2.5i	19,720	19,720	0.0
Subaru Impreza WRX TR (manual)	24,620	24,620	0.0
Toyota Camry LE 4-cyl.	22,065	21,080	-4.5
Toyota Corolla LE	17,545	17,910	2.1
Toyota Matrix	19,260	19,260	0.0
Toyota Prius	23,490	23,780	1.2

* Consumer Reports "recommended" 2007 cars under $25,000 that have been recommended for 2 years in a row. Includes destination fee and optional equipment.

---

some extent, these improvements are reflected in rising sticker prices.

Sometimes you have a choice of whether or not to buy improvements, while other times you do not. Some improvements are a product of the marketplace, where automakers seeking profits and market share compete with each other for customers who are seeking the best quality they can afford. Other improvements are made because the Government mandates them (for example, many safety and antipollution features).

It is not easy to calculate the genuine value to consumers of some quality improvements, especially where the buyer's only choice is to "take it or leave it." Nonetheless, each year the Government tries to estimate their value—that is, how much they add to the price of a new car. Table 3 shows these estimates for the period 1973 through 2007, with a breakdown showing how much of the increase in new car prices is due to new safety equipment, better emissions control and fuel economy, and other quality improvements.

Table 2b
2006 vs. 2007 M.S.R.P. FOR SELECTED MODELS*

Model	2006 M.S.R.P.	2007 M.S.R.P.	Percent Change
Honda CR-V EX (AWD)	24,300	24,645	1.4
Honda Element EX (AWD)	22,240	23,705	6.6
Jeep Liberty Sport (V6, 4WD)	24,310	24,310	0.0
Subaru Forester 2.5 X	23,220	23,420	0.9

* Consumer Reports "recommended" 2007 trucks, minivans and SUVs under $25,000 that have been recommended for 2 years in a row. Includes destination fee and optional equipment.

Quality improvements help explain why the sticker price of a Honda Accord (V6), for example, has increased from roughly $12,000 in 1990 to $25,000 today. They also help explain the more recent price increases shown in Tables 2a and 2b. However, these figures may overstate the increase in the prices that car buyers actually pay. Few car buyers actually pay the M.S.R.P.—and in recent years they have enjoyed especially large discounts. Car manufacturers have been trying to keep their sales rates up by offering various rebates and incentives. For example, last summer DaimlerChrysler offered employee pricing to the general public on most of their models. Many manufacturers also offer zero percent financing or cash allowances as well as bonus cash to new college graduates and the military.

The size of the discounts depends on the model. If a car is so popular that dealers are all but sold out, you may have to pay the full M.S.R.P. Indeed, if a car is exceptionally scarce relative to the demand for it, you may pay *more* than the M.S.R.P. An example is the Toyota Camry Hybrid, for which there still remains a months' long waiting list in some areas of the country. These "popularity premiums," it should be noted, usually are fleeting. They typically disappear within a year, after which the asking price usually falls back down to the M.S.R.P. or even lower. Hence, if you are tempted to pay a premium for a popular car, be aware that it might not carry over proportionately to the subsequent resale value of the vehicle.

How long will car makers continue to offer large financial incentives? Possibly for a long time. Since they first began offering them a few years ago, they have periodically tried to cut back. Each time, car sales have weakened—and the incentives have been sweetened again.

It is also possible, however, that car makers will try to recapture some of the profit that they lose through rebates by raising their sticker prices.

In other words, you may be able to get $4,000 off the M.S.R.P., but the M.S.R.P. may have been raised to offset some of this discount. In any case, you should always keep in mind that, from the buyer's perspective, any advertised incentive should be regarded as only a *starting point* for negotiation.

Table 3
AVERAGE ADDED COSTS FOR NEW CAR QUALITY ADJUSTMENTS

Model Year	Safety	Emissions[1]	Other[2]	Total
1973	$218.06	$70.56	$26.75	$315.37
1974	259.43	3.38	21.46	284.27
1975	23.75	264.55	0.00	288.30
1976	27.96	15.86	-11.27	32.55
1977	13.78	28.36	75.15	117.29
1978	0.00	18.40	73.91	92.31
1979	9.81	20.65	48.64	79.10
1980	20.99	186.41	173.99	381.39
1981	6.39	695.24	89.26	790.89
1982	0.00	121.37	59.68	181.05
1983	0.00	90.34	88.58	178.92
1984	-16.42	79.97	85.93	149.48
1985	0.00	26.41	172.86	199.27
1986	34.61	0.00	200.79	235.40
1987	0.00	0.00	57.41	57.41
1988	78.12	0.00	215.12	293.24
1989	27.11	0.00	187.08	214.19
1990	205.26	0.00	44.41	249.67
1991	239.60	0.00	0.00	239.60
1992	37.68	0.00	244.77	282.45
1993	0.00	0.00	94.59	94.59
1994	188.94	40.50	143.81	373.25
1995	120.36	53.74	0.00	174.10
1996	16.31	87.23	86.90	190.44
1997	8.97	20.45	153.35	182.77
1998	0.00	51.73	177.27	229.00
1999	0.00	76.61	408.25	484.86
2000	15.26	0.00	0.00	15.26
2001	25.16	67.65	0.00	92.81
2002	n.a.	n.a.	n.a.	68.30
2003	n.a.	n.a.	n.a.	25.08
2004	37.16	0.00	45.80	82.96
2005	193.11	0.00	117.39	310.50
2006	0.00	26.79	2.45	29.24
2007	56.57	0.00	94.34	150.91

[1] Includes changes to improve fuel economy and emissions control. [2] Includes improved warranties, corrosion protection and changes in standard equipment. n.a. = not available.

Source: Bureau of Labor Statistics, *Quality Changes for Vehicles 2007*.

In many cases you may be able to negotiate an even greater discount.

Another factor that influences car prices is the exchange rate of the U.S. dollar against foreign currencies. When the dollar's exchange value drops, as it has throughout much of the previous 12 months, foreign manufacturers have two choices: they can raise the dollar price of their cars to make up for the dollar's loss of value, or they can try to "absorb" some of the dollar's decrease and hold the dollar prices of their cars down as far as possible, in order to remain competitive. In today's highly competitive market, they usually they try to hold their dollar prices down as long as possible.

Currency fluctuations, however, have less of an impact on motor vehicle prices now than they did in the past. This is because Japanese and European car makers increasingly are relying on "transplant production," *i.e.*, building their cars and trucks in the United States. Most of the moderately-priced Japanese vehicles that are sold here are now made here. Toyota, for example, currently has several factories in North America, most within the United States, and plans to build two more; by 2008 Toyota expects to have the capacity to build nearly 2 million cars and trucks a year at these plants. (It is ironic that the increase in foreign auto production in the United States largely is attributable to the quotas and tariffs that U.S. automakers lobbied for precisely to avoid such competition.)

Yet another trend that is influencing the prices that car buyers pay is the growing use of the Internet to gather information before purchasing a vehicle. Consumers can now easily get model information, crash-test results and other safety information, read vehicle reviews, find invoice prices for new cars and published values for used cars, utilize car-buying and dealer-referral services, and shop for financing and insurance. It seems likely that the increased "transparency" in invoice prices, in particular, has enhanced the ability of consumers to negotiate, and probably will continue to do so.

In sum, improved quality among manufacturers and an increasingly competitive pricing environment should continue to benefit consumers. Moreover, with well over one hundred models of cars, SUVs, and pickup trucks available on showroom floors this year, there are more choices than ever. The bottom line is this: Except for some vehicles experiencing strong demand, car shoppers are currently enjoying a buyers' market.

Financing

For many car buyers, an additional cost is the amount of interest that must be paid on a car loan. A *Consumer Reports* financing study reveals that "a bad financing deal can cost $2,700 more than a good one." If you plan to purchase a car on credit and interest rates drop, the lower "price" of borrowed funds can "offset" the higher purchase price of cars. Conversely, higher interest rates can offset decreases in new car prices.

No one can predict what levels interest rates may achieve over the next year or so. Some cars are available with rates as low as zero percent, with payments stretched out as long as 72 months. Sometimes the manufacturers offer these cut-rate loans only to buyers who are willing to forego a cash rebate—an option that buyers who need the rebates as down payments for their new cars are unlikely to choose. Keep in mind that rebates or low-cost financing incentives should have no bearing on your negotiations, because the manufacturer offers them, not the dealer. (Dealers often receive their own reimbursements and incentives from manufacturers.)

Whether the combination of changes in purchase prices and interest rates results in a net increase or decrease in the overall costs of acquiring a given new car in any year depends, of course, on how much prices increased or decreased and how far the interest rate dropped or rose.

How to Figure the "Worth" of Interest-Rate Differences and Cash Rebates

Table 4 on pages 58-59 shows the "worth" or "cost" to you of interest-rate differences (either on loans from your bank or on special interest-rate dealer financing) per $1,000 borrowed on standard 2-,3-,4-, and 5-year car loans. You can use the table to compare the "savings" you might realize by taking a loan at a below-market rate. You also can use it to compare the value of a below-market loan with a cash rebate—the two choices that dealers are most likely to offer as incentives. Determining what interest-rate differences and cash rebates actually are "worth" to you could be an important part of your decision to purchase a particular new car.

For example, suppose you are planning to borrow $15,000 to finance the purchase of a new car. A car dealer offers you a 48-month loan at four percent. How much could you save if you could get the loan for three percent? According to the table, over four years the lower-rate loan would save you $19.31 per $1,000 borrowed. Thus, on a $15,000 loan you would save $289.65. (If you invested the monthly savings as you went along, you would save even more.)

As another example, suppose your car dealer offers you a choice between a $1,500 cash rebate or a low-rate short-term loan, say, two percent interest over two years. Furthermore, suppose you need to borrow $15,000, and your bank is willing to make the same loan at six percent interest. According to the table, by taking the loan at two percent rather than six percent, over two years you would save $40.58 per $1,000 borrowed. On a $15,000 loan your savings would be $608.70 ($40.58 multiplied by 15). On balance, the rebate is the better deal.

Some banks and credit unions now offer the option of refinancing a car loan. The best refinancing rates are available on shorter-length loans and to customers with good credit. However, if you consider refinancing, avoid stretching out the payments beyond the term left on your existing loan. Match the length of your new loan to the number of months left on your current loan (or less), so that, despite a lower interest rate, you do not end up paying more in total interest.

Hybrids

Once enamored with large SUVs, today more and more car buyers are turning away from these gas guzzlers toward the new fuel efficient gas/electric hybrid vehicles. Previously just a curiosity, a combination of rising gas prices, tax incentives, and an increasing concern about American consumption of foreign oil are helping push hybrid cars into the mainstream.

Although hybrids only accounted for 1.5 percent of car sales in 2006, demand for them is growing. Until recently, waiting lists for purchases of new hybrids extended out for several months. For example, wait lists for early models of the Toyota Prius were nearly one year long in some areas. However, recent production has increased to meet demand for most models and waiting lists for most hybrids have shrunk or disappeared. Most manufacturers now offer, or have plans to offer, hybrid vehicles.

It varies considerably by model, but hybrids do get better gas mileage than their gasoline only counterparts. For example, based on EPA estimates (using their old methodology) the gasoline powered Honda Civic is rated at 30 MPG city and 40 MPG highway while the hybrid version of the car is rated 49 MPG city and 51 MPG highway (these are official estimates; many hybrid owners have reported lower fuel efficiency than the EPA's estimates). Note that starting with 2008 model year vehicles, the EPA has changed the way it calculates MPG. The new MPG estimates will be lower

Table 4
SAVINGS PER $1,000 BORROWED AT DIFFERENT INTEREST RATES

Loan Period (In Months)	Lower Rate	2%	3%	4%	5%	6%	*Higher Rate* 7%	8%	9%	10%	11%	12%	13%
24	1%	$9.99	$20.04	$30.15	$40.33	$50.57	$60.87	$71.24	$81.66	$92.15	$102.70	$113.32	$123.99
	2%		10.05	20.16	30.34	40.58	50.88	61.25	71.67	82.16	92.72	103.33	114.01
	3%			10.11	20.29	30.53	40.83	51.20	61.62	72.11	82.66	93.28	103.95
	4%				10.18	20.42	30.72	41.08	51.51	62.00	72.55	83.16	93.84
	5%					10.24	20.54	30.91	41.33	51.82	62.37	72.99	83.66
	6%						10.30	20.67	31.09	51.58	52.13	62.75	73.42
	7%							10.36	20.79	31.28	41.83	52.45	63.12
	8%								10.43	20.92	31.47	42.08	52.76
	9%									10.49	21.04	31.65	42.33
	10%										10.55	21.17	31.84
	11%											10.61	21.29
	12%												10.68
36	1%	$14.50	$29.13	$43.91	$58.82	$73.87	$89.05	$104.38	$119.84	$135.43	$151.17	$167.04	$183.04
	2%		14.64	29.41	44.32	59.37	74.56	89.88	105.34	120.94	136.67	152.54	168.54
	3%			14.77	29.69	44.73	59.92	75.24	90.71	106.30	122.04	137.90	153.91
	4%				14.91	29.96	45.15	60.47	75.93	91.53	107.26	123.13	139.13
	5%					15.05	30.24	45.56	61.02	76.62	92.35	108.22	124.22
	6%						15.19	30.51	45.97	61.57	77.30	93.17	109.17
	7%							15.32	30.78	46.38	62.11	77.98	93.99
	8%								15.46	31.06	46.79	62.66	78.66
	9%									15.60	31.33	47.20	63.20
	10%										15.73	31.60	47.61
	11%											15.87	31.87
	12%												16.00

Note: Figures represent present value using a discount factor of 5 percent.

Loan Period (In Months) 48

Lower Rate	2%	3%	4%	5%	6%	7%	8%	9%	10%	11%	12%	13%
1%	$18.83	$37.90	$57.21	$76.76	$96.55	$116.58	$136.85	$157.35	$178.08	$199.05	$220.26	$241.69
2%		19.07	38.38	57.93	77.72	97.75	118.01	138.52	159.25	180.22	201.43	222.86
3%			19.31	38.86	58.65	78.68	98.94	119.44	140.18	161.15	182.36	203.79
4%				19.55	39.34	59.37	79.63	100.13	120.87	141.84	163.04	184.48
5%					19.79	39.82	60.08	80.58	101.32	122.29	143.49	164.93
6%						20.03	40.29	60.79	81.53	102.50	123.70	145.14
7%							20.26	40.77	61.50	82.47	103.68	125.11
8%								20.50	41.24	62.21	83.41	104.85
9%									20.74	41.71	62.91	84.35
10%										20.97	42.17	63.61
11%											21.20	42.64
12%												21.44

Loan Period (In Months) 60

Lower Rate	2%	3%	4%	5%	6%	7%	8%	9%	10%	11%	12%	13%
1%	$23.00	$46.36	$70.09	$94.19	$118.65	$143.47	$168.65	$194.19	$220.09	$246.34	$272.94	$299.89
2%		23.37	47.10	71.19	95.65	120.47	145.65	171.19	197.09	223.34	249.94	276.89
3%			23.73	47.83	72.29	97.11	122.29	147.83	173.72	199.97	226.58	253.53
4%				24.10	48.55	73.37	98.56	124.10	149.99	176.24	202.84	229.80
5%					24.46	49.28	74.46	100.00	125.90	152.15	178.75	205.70
6%						24.82	50.00	75.54	101.44	127.69	154.29	181.24
7%							25.18	50.72	76.62	102.87	129.47	156.42
8%								25.54	51.44	77.69	104.29	131.24
9%									25.90	52.15	78.75	105.70
10%										26.25	52.85	79.81
11%											26.60	53.56
12%												26.95

Note: Figures represent present value using a discount factor of 5 percent.

than old estimates to account for the faster speeds and acceleration of typical drivers, the common use of air conditioning, and increased operation in cold temperatures. For example, the MPG ratings for the 2007 Civic under the new guidelines are 25 MPG city and 36 MPG highway.

Despite the higher gas mileage of hybrid vehicles, studies have found that they still cost more to own and operate than their conventional equivalents. This is partly because hybrid purchase prices range from roughly $3,000 to $9,000 more than their gasoline counterparts. Hybrids also depreciate faster and incur extra sales taxes and financing costs. Fuel savings would have to increase substantially over current levels (in some cases over *five times* more) to compensate for these added costs.

To illustrate, the Honda Accord (estimated combined MPG of 23) sells for around $25,000 while a comparable Accord Hybrid (estimated combined MPG of 31) retails for roughly $30,600. Assuming 15,000 miles driven per year, and a $3.00 gas price, after five years of ownership fuel cost savings make up only $2,525 of the $5,600 price difference (or $4,300 with the $1,300 tax credit available on this model—see below). Ignoring the time value of money, the Accord Hybrid would have to get 53.8 MPG for its cost to be comparable to the gas model. Alternatively, at current MPG estimates, individuals would have to drive 33,273 miles or more per year to save more by owning the hybrid.

As part of the Energy Policy Act of 2005, the federal government is trying to steer potential car buyers toward hybrids by offering a tax credit on the purchase of qualified hybrids. This *tax credit* replaces the previous clean-fuel burning *tax deduction* and applies to all new hybrid cars purchased or placed in service on or after January 1, 2006.

The size of the tax credit varies by model and is determined by a two-part calculation done by the IRS. The first part, called the "conservation credit," is determined by how much fuel the vehicle saves over 120,000 miles of driving when compared to its weight class in 2002. Oddly enough, a vehicle that uses more gas over its lifespan, but is in a class that has poor fuel economy, can get a higher conservation credit than a vehicle that uses less gas over its lifespan but is in a class that already has good fuel economy.

The second part of the tax credit, called the "fuel economy credit," is based on the vehicle's improved fuel economy when compared to the fuel economy of its weight class in the 2002 model year. The combined maximum available credit for any vehicle is $3,400. The Toyota Prius currently has the largest credit ($3,150) while the GMC Sierra Hybrid (2WD) and the Chevrolet Silverado Hybrid (2WD) have the lowest ($250).

The tax credit begins a one-year phase out for each manufacturer after they sell their 60,000th qualified hybrid vehicle. The phase out begins in the calendar quarter after the quarter when the 60,000th vehicle was sold. At this point the credit is cut to half the original credit. This reduced credit lasts for the next two quarters. After that, the credit is cut again by half to a quarter of the original credit. This continues for another two quarters, after which the tax credit expires. All tax credits, regardless of the number of vehicles sold, expire after 2010.

To qualify for the credit, not only does the hybrid need to be approved by the IRS, but the vehicle cannot be purchased for resale and has to be driven primarily in the United States. The rules are not yet clear as to what happens if you purchase a hybrid, take the credit, and later decide to sell the car. If you do, you may end up having to give back some or all of the credit. Also, if you lease a hybrid, the credit goes to the leasing company, not you.

Due in large part to sales of the popular Prius, as of August 2006 Toyota/Lexus was the only manufacturer to have crossed the 60,000 vehicle threshold. Since they sold their 60,000th hybrid in the third quarter of 2006, starting October 1, 2006, the beginning of the fourth quarter, the tax credits on **all** Toyota/Lexus vehicles were halved and were halved again on April 1, 2007. They expired in full on September 30, 2007. A complete list of qualified hybrids, their credit amounts and their expiration schedule is available online at www.fueleconomy.gov/feg/tax_hybrid.shtml.

There are incentives for hybrids at the state level as well. Connecticut, for example, does not require sales tax on hybrid purchases if the vehicle is rated over 40 miles per gallon. Other states, such a Virginia and Georgia, allow qualified hybrid vehicles to travel in the High Occupancy Vehicle (HOV) lane regardless of the number of passengers. Some cities even offer free parking for hybrids. For some drivers these perks, like getting home earlier because you can travel faster in the HOV lane, may more than offset the extra cost of the hybrid.

The Extended Outlook

The extended outlook for new car markets appears favorable for American consumers. Cars and trucks are more comfortable, better equipped, safer, cleaner, and more reliable than ever. Warranties and service contracts are becoming more generous. Moreover, vehicles are also more affordable owing to low interest rates, stiff competition among manufacturers and dealers, and economies of scale attributable to the globalization of vehicle production and sales.

Excess capacity will continue to spur global consolidation and restructuring among manufacturers. Some analysts predict that consolidation may continue to whittle down the number of auto makers. These trends will allow producers to cut costs, share technology, and facilitate marketing.

Car buyers now have ready access to a wealth of information over the Internet, such as model specifications, prices, safety tests, reliability, financing, insurance, reviews, advice, and more. In response to price conscious shoppers, some dealers have adopted more consumer friendly sales tactics such as one-price selling. Buyers who do not want to bargain on their own can even hire a shopper to do it for them. At bottom, dealerships that cling to the traditional "hard-sell" approach may find it difficult to sell to increasingly savvy customers.

The continuing trend toward reduced trade barriers and greater adoption and application of technology will lead to fewer competitors, but increased competition; lower manufacturing and distribution costs; safer, more reliable, and more efficient cars; and an unprecedented amount of information to help car buyers make good decisions and get better deals. This means that, for the foreseeable future, car shoppers should continue to enjoy a buyer's market.

IV.

SHOULD YOU BUY NEW OR USED?

THE high volume of new car sales in recent years, spurred by attractive sales incentives, has created a bumper crop of late-model used cars. Millions of cars are traded in every year, many of them with relatively low mileage. In addition, millions of vehicles are returned to dealer lots each year when their leases expire. Because of stipulations in the contract, leased cars are usually well kept and in much better condition than the fleet cars that used-car buyers had to settle for in the past.

Not only do used-car buyers have a wider range of cars to choose from, but the cars are not physically depreciating as fast as they did years ago. Presumably, this is partly due to the better build of cars generally, the higher quality of previously leased cars on the market, and the fact that leases limit the number of miles someone can drive a car without adding cost to the lease.

The glut of used cars, coupled with improvements in quality, mean that it is possible to get a good deal on a late-model used car. For example, our tables show that the 2004 Ford Taurus, one of *Consumer Reports*' recommended used cars, currently sells for just 47 percent of its original M.S.R.P. The 2003 Buick LeSabre, which is also recommended, is selling for 41 percent of its original sticker price. As noted earlier, the percentages in our tables on pages 15-49 should be interpreted with caution. In some instances, they probably exaggerate the drop in price for some cars. Conversely, they probably understate the drop for others. Nonetheless, they provide at least some indication of what dealers are asking today for used cars compared with what they were asking when the cars were new. By all reports, they are asking substantially less.

The trend toward longer warranties also has made used cars more attractive. The standard bumper-to-bumper warranty used to run for three years or 36,000 miles. But some automakers now offer them for four years and 50,000 miles, or even longer. Powertrain warranties, which cover the car's engine and transmission, may run as long as ten years or 100,000 miles. In addition, many warranties can be transferred from one owner to the next (check before you buy a used car). Some used cars that have been "certified" by car makers carry additional warranties (for example, Toyota's certified vehicles carry a seven-year, 100,000 limited factory warranty).

In today's market, used-car buyers probably will find it relatively easy to find a "recommended" late-model car selling at a good discount from its original price. Even if you can afford a new car, the current "low" resale prices of cars would seem to favor used-car purchases over new-car purchases. Of course, there still are bargains to be had on new cars. Whether buying new or used, we recommend that car shoppers consult the April auto issue of *Consumer Reports*, which lists new and used cars that are "good bets."

Useful Information

If you have decided to buy a new car, there are a number of consumer services that provide price information. Ascertaining the actual dealer cost (and manufacturer rebate or dealer holdback, if any) of the vehicle you want gives you an important advantage when it comes time to "deal" for price; that is, you know what the difference between the sticker price and the dealer's actual cost is. That amount—sometimes thousands of dollars—is negotiable. If you let the salesperson know at the outset that you have obtained the dealer cost, you are much more apt to arrive swiftly at a mutually acceptable price than if you walk into the showroom uninformed. Remember when bargaining to negotiate from the dealer cost up, not from the M.S.R.P. down. Typically, you can buy most vehicles for four to eight percent over invoice. Expect to get a better deal on less popular models and to pay more for vehicles in high demand.

Consumer Reports offers a computerized price and options printout for most new cars. To order a printout you can call (800) 888-8275. The cost is $14 for the first car report, and $12 for each additional report ordered at the same time. The 10-20 page report, available by fax, mail, or online, includes invoice prices for all factory-installed options and packages; current national rebates, unadvertised dealer incentives and holdbacks; safety ratings, and more. *Consumer Reports* also provides reports on *used* cars. The phone number is (800) 258-1169 and the cost is $12 for a report that includes price estimates, a reliability summary, and negotiating tips. We assume that the price information is the same as that in the *N.A.D.A. Official Used Car Guide*.

On the web, Edmunds (www.edmunds.com), Kelley Blue Book (www.kbb.com), and the N.A.D.A. (www.nadaguides.com) provide pricing information on new and used cars, as well as a host of other buying information (such as reviews and the latest rebates and incentives). Of course, every manufacturer and nearly all dealers have their own websites. CARFAX (www.carfax.com) and AutoCheck (www.autocheck.com) provide history reports that reveal whether a vehicle has been totaled or salvaged, experienced flood damages, or had other problems that may affect its safety or resale value.

At the website of the National Highway Traffic Safety Administration, www.nhtsa.gov, you can find front and side impact crash test results and "rollover resistance" ratings, as well as information on recalls, defects, and consumer complaints for each model. To see only the rollover ratings, go to www.safercar.gov. The Insurance Institute for Highway Safety provides additional crash test results at its website, www.iihs.org.

AIER is not connected in any way with any of these organizations or websites but we believe the services they offer may be valuable to car buyers.

Used Car Best Buys

If you decide to shop for a used car, there is a simple way to determine which ones may be the best buys. As we mentioned in Chapter II, some cars that have been judged roadworthy by independent auto analysts have depreciated in dollar value much more rapidly than others. Clearly, if you are thinking of buying a *new* car, you want to buy one that will retain its resale value as long as possible, and therefore you would avoid those cars that depreciate quickly, even if they have been tested and found to be mechanically reliable. On the other hand, if you are shopping for a *used* car, that is precisely the kind of car that can offer the best value. That is, you can obtain inexpensive reliable transportation by choosing a "recommended" model that depreciated faster than most others. Among the cars listed at the *bottom of the rankings* in the tables on pages 15-49 there are some good used-car buys.

In Tables 5-9, we have listed in increasing order *Consumer Reports'* recommended used vehicles according to their resale values expressed as a percent of the original M.S.R.P. As shown, there are very substantial differences in the extent to which different makes and models depreciated in dollar value.

We have also shown the resale value as an approximate percent of the cost of purchasing a similar 2007 model. Any of the vehicles that either depreciated more than other recommended models, or whose resale prices are a relatively small percent of the current cost of purchasing a similar new model, are probably good buys. The vehicles with resale prices that show both of the above characteristics are probably the "best buys."

To illustrate, say you are interested in a used midsize car. In Table 6, listing model-year 2003 recommended used cars, there are two such cars that are roughly the same size and in the same price range—the 2003 Mitsubishi Galant and the 2003 Honda Accord. Which is the better value (relative to its original and present new car price)? The Mitsubishi Galant appears near the top of both columns whereas the Honda Accord is listed near the bottom of both columns. The average retail value of a 2003 Mitsubishi Galant in September 2007, $7,519, was $10,248 less than the original manufacturer's price, and $12,380 less than the 2007 manufacturer's suggested retail price for a comparable new Galant (the 2007 Galant has a sticker price of $19,899).

Compare those differences with the Honda Accord. The $15,775 average retail value of a 2003 Honda Accord was $7,225 less than the original M.S.R.P. and $7,575 less than the M.S.R.P. for a 2007 model. The Galant not only has a lower price than the Accord, but in terms of price relative to what the cars originally cost (42 percent vs. 69 percent) and what it would cost to replace them with a new model (38 percent vs. 68 percent), the Galant provides "more car" for the money than does the Accord.

Table 5
COMPARISON OF 2002 "RECOMMENDED" USED VEHICLE*
NADA RETAIL VALUES
(September 2007)

As % of Original M.S.R.P.		As % of 2007 M.S.R.P.†	
Lincoln Continental	26.6	Lincoln Town Car	27.2
Lincoln Town Car	32.4	Acura RL	33.0
Buick Century	34.0	Ford Crown Victoria	36.0
Acura RL	37.2	Mercury Grand Marquis	37.6
Mazda Millenia	38.1	Hyundai Sante Fe	37.8
Mercury Grand Marquis	38.8	Mitsubishi Eclipse	41.5
Ford Crown Victoria	39.0	Lexus LS	42.1
Infiniti I35	44.0	Nissan Xterra	42.3
Infiniti QX4	44.8	Volvo S60 (FWD)	42.5
Chevrolet Tracker	46.3	Lexus LX	43.8
Chevrolet Prizm	46.5	Lexus GS	44.7
Infiniti G20	47.0	Toyota Land Cruiser	44.8
Lexus LS	47.2	Acura MDX	45.2
Lexus LX	47.7	Chevrolet Silverado (2WD)	45.8
Toyota Land Cruiser	47.9	Lexus SC	46.3
Volvo S60 (FWD)	48.4	Suzuki Grand Vitara	46.8
Suzuki Grand Vitara	48.8	Honda Civic	47.0
Toyota Sienna	49.3	Toyota Sienna	48.7
Lexus SC	49.6	Subaru Forester	49.2
Mitsubishi Eclipse	49.8	Toyota Camry Solara	49.5
Subaru Legacy Outback	50.5	Lexus RX	49.6
Subaru Outback	51.4	GMC Sierra 1500 (2WD)	49.7
Toyota Avalon	51.7	Toyota Avalon	49.7
Acura MDX	52.1	Toyota Corolla	50.2
Hyundai Sante Fe	53.0	Lexus IS	50.6
Subaru Forester	53.3	Ford Mustang (V6)	50.8
Lexus GS	53.3	Lexus ES	51.1
Nissan Xterra	54.2	Honda S2000	51.6
Lexus ES	54.3	Mazda MX-5 Miata	51.8
Honda Accord	54.3	Nissan Altima	52.1
Honda S2000	54.6	Honda Accord	52.6
Mazda Protégé	55.0	Toyota Tundra	53.6
Saturn SL	55.8	Toyota Prius	53.9
Lexus RX	56.6	Ford F-250 (4WD)	54.3
Ford Mustang (V6)	56.9	BMW 3 Series (AWD)	56.5
Mazda MX-5 Miata	58.1	Toyota Highlander	56.6
Lexus IS	59.0	Honda CR-V	56.8
Toyota Highlander	59.0	Nissan Frontier	58.2
Toyota Prius	59.7	Subaru Outback	58.5
Toyota Corolla	60.3	Ford F-150	59.5
Subaru Impreza	61.9	Subaru Impreza	60.2
Toyota Camry Solara	62.1	Toyota 4Runner	60.4
Toyota 4Runner	63.4	Subaru Legacy Outback	61.9
GMC Sierra 1500 (2WD)	63.5	Toyota Camry	62.0
Toyota Camry	63.8	Toyota RAV4	64.8
Nissan Altima	64.6	Toyota Tacoma	84.3

Table 5 (Continued)
COMPARISON OF 2002 "RECOMMENDED" USED VEHICLE*
NADA RETAIL VALUES
(September 2007)

As % of Original M.S.R.P.		As % of 2007 M.S.R.P.†	
Acura RSX	64.8	Lincoln Continental	n.a.
Ford F-250 (4WD)	66.4	Buick Century	n.a.
BMW Z3	67.1	Mazda Millenia	n.a.
Honda CR-V	69.1	Infiniti I35	n.a.
Ford F-150	69.2	Infiniti QX4	n.a.
Chevrolet Silverado (2WD)	69.6	Chevrolet Tracker	n.a.
Toyota Celica	70.9	Chevrolet Prizm	n.a.
Toyota Echo	70.9	Infiniti G20	n.a.
Honda Civic	71.6	Mazda Protégé	n.a.
Toyota Tundra	76.5	Saturn SL	n.a.
BMW 3 Series (AWD)	77.4	Acura RSX	n.a.
Nissan Frontier	78.7	BMW Z3	n.a.
Toyota RAV4	82.1	Toyota Celica	n.a.
Toyota Tacoma	100.5	Toyota Echo	n.a.

* From *Consumer Reports* list of "reliable used vehicles," April 2007. † Same or comparable new model. na Indicates no comparable model available..

Table 6
COMPARISON OF 2003 "RECOMMENDED" USED VEHICLE*
NADA RETAIL VALUES
(September 2007)

As % of Original M.S.R.P.		As % of 2007 M.S.R.P.†	
Buick LeSabre	40.5	Mitsubishi Galant	37.8
Ford Taurus	41.4	Acura RL	39.2
Buick Regal	42.3	Hyundai Sonata	40.2
Mitsubishi Galant	42.3	Ford Crown Victoria	40.7
Ford Crown Victoria	43.7	Mercury Grand Marquis	44.4
Acura RL	44.3	Hyundai Sante Fe	45.3
Mercury Sable	44.8	Nissan Maxima	47.9
Mercury Grand Marquis	45.9	Lexus LS	48.3
Hyundai Sonata	47.5	Nissan Xterra	49.2
Pontiac Grand Prix	50.0	Pontiac Grand Prix	49.3
Infiniti QX4	52.7	Jeep Liberty	49.6
Chevrolet Monte Carlo (V6)	52.8	Subaru Impreza WRX	49.7
Infiniti I35	53.1	Chevrolet Monte Carlo (V6)	51.4
Mazda B-Series (4WD)	53.5	Mazda B-Series (4WD)	51.7
Lexus LS	53.6	Infiniti FX	51.7
Nissan Maxima	53.9	Lexus SC	52.6
Lexus SC	55.5	Lexus GS	52.9
Subaru Outback	58.9	Mitsubishi Outlander	53.0
Toyota Land Cruiser	59.0	Ford Explorer Sport Trac	54.2
Toyota Sienna	59.3	Honda Civic Hybrid	54.3
Lexus LX	59.6	Acura MDX	55.0
Subaru Impreza WRX	60.9	Ford Ranger (4WD)	55.4
Honda S2000	61.5	BMW Z4	55.5
Acura MDX	61.6	Lexus LX	55.8
Toyota Avalon	61.9	Toyota Land Cruiser	56.0
Lexus ES	62.6	Honda Civic	57.0
Honda Civic Hybrid	62.8	Lexus RX	57.6
Hyundai Sante Fe	62.9	Lexus IS	57.8
Mitsubishi Outlander	63.0	Toyota Camry Solara	58.1
Lexus GS	63.0	Mazda MX-5 Miata	58.1
Honda Odyssey	63.0	Honda S2000	58.5
Nissan Xterra	63.2	Toyota Sienna	58.7
BMW 3 Series Convertible	63.4	Lexus ES	59.2
Lexus RX	63.6	Nissan Altima	59.2
Mazda MX-5 Miata	63.9	Toyota Avalon	59.5
Honda Pilot	65.1	Honda Odyssey	60.0
Subaru Baja	65.1	Subaru Forester	61.2
Ford Explorer Sport Trac	65.2	Toyota Tundra	62.2
Subaru Forester	65.6	Toyota Highlander	63.6
Toyota Highlander	66.3	Honda CR-V	64.1
Mazda Protégé	67.2	Toyota Prius	64.4
Lexus IS	67.3	Honda Pilot	64.6
Pontiac Vibe	67.4	Pontiac Vibe	65.7
BMW Z4	67.7	Nissan Frontier	65.9
Lexus GX	68.4	Lexus GX	65.9
Honda Accord	68.6	Subaru Legacy	66.7

Table 6 (Continued)
COMPARISON OF 2003 "RECOMMENDED" USED VEHICLE*
NADA RETAIL VALUES
(September 2007)

As % of Original M.S.R.P.		As % of 2007 M.S.R.P.†	
Subaru Legacy	70.1	Honda Element	66.8
Toyota Camry Solara	70.2	Ford F-150	67.1
Toyota Prius	71.4	Toyota Corolla	67.5
Toyota Camry	71.7	Honda Accord	67.6
Nissan Altima	72.1	Ford F-250 (2WD)	67.8
Ford F-250 (2WD)	72.4	BMW 3 Series Coupe	67.9
Jeep Liberty	72.6	Subaru Outback	68.3
Subaru Impreza	72.7	Toyota Camry	69.7
Toyota 4Runner	73.3	Toyota Matrix	70.2
Acura RSX	74.1	Subaru Impreza	71.1
Ford F-150	75.2	Toyota 4Runner	72.2
Infiniti FX	75.4	Toyota RAV4	72.6
Ford Ranger (4WD)	75.9	BMW 3 Series Convertible	80.0
Toyota Corolla	76.3	Toyota Tacoma	91.8
Honda CR-V	77.6	Buick LeSabre	n.a.
Toyota Matrix	77.6	Ford Taurus	n.a.
Toyota Echo	81.6	Buick Regal	n.a.
Honda Element	81.8	Mercury Sable	n.a.
Toyota Celica	82.2	Infiniti QX4	n.a.
BMW 3 Series Coupe	86.3	Infiniti I35	n.a.
Honda Civic	86.8	Subaru Baja	n.a.
Toyota Tundra	86.9	Mazda Protégé	n.a.
Nissan Frontier	87.9	Acura RSX	n.a.
Toyota RAV4	92.0	Toyota Echo	n.a.
Toyota Tacoma	107.5	Toyota Celica	n.a.

* From *Consumer Reports* list of "reliable used vehicles," April 2007. † Same or comparable new model. na Indicates no comparable model available..

Table 7
COMPARISON OF 2004 "RECOMMENDED" USED VEHICLE* NADA RETAIL VALUES
(September 2007)

As % of Original M.S.R.P.		As % of 2007 M.S.R.P.†	
Buick Century	44.2	Lincoln Town Car	42.8
Buick LeSabre	45.9	Ford Crown Victoria	44.5
Ford Crown Victoria	46.4	Acura RL	45.3
Ford Taurus	47.2	Hyundai Sonata	46.1
Mercury Sable	48.7	Volvo S80	49.9
Lincoln Town Car	49.4	Mercury Grand Marquis	50.6
Buick Regal	50.0	Volvo V70	51.2
Acura RL	51.0	Nissan Pathfinder	52.9
Mercury Grand Marquis	52.6	Hyundai Sante Fe	54.4
Hyundai Sonata	52.8	Jeep Liberty	56.1
Volvo S80	54.5	Hyundai Elantra	56.9
Buick Rendezvous	56.5	Infiniti FX	57.3
Pontiac Grand Prix	57.6	Pontiac Grand Prix	57.4
Infiniti I35	59.1	Lexus LS	58.9
Chevrolet Monte Carlo (V6)	61.3	Toyota Sequoia	59.8
Hyundai Elantra	61.6	Mazda B-Series (4WD)	60.6
Lexus SC	64.4	Lexus GS	60.7
Subaru Legacy Outback	64.7	Mitsubishi Outlander	61.2
Lexus LS	65.2	Lexus SC	61.5
Mazda B-Series (4WD)	66.0	Chevrolet Monte Carlo (V6)	61.7
Nissan Pathfinder	66.5	Ford Ranger (4WD)	62.4
Lexus LX	67.2	Lexus LX	64.0
Toyota Land Cruiser	67.6	Honda Civic	65.1
Subaru Outback	69.0	Toyota Land Cruiser	65.2
Honda S2000	69.1	Honda Civic Hybrid	65.5
Subaru Impreza WRX	69.9	Nissan Altima	65.6
Toyota Avalon	70.2	Mazda MX-5 Miata	65.9
Mazda MX-5 Miata	71.5	Acura MDX	66.1
Lexus GS	72.3	Honda S2000	66.2
Acura MDX	72.6	Lexus IS	66.6
Lexus ES	72.9	Toyota Camry Solara	66.8
Hyundai Sante Fe	73.0	Infiniti G35 Sedan (AWD)	68.0
Honda Odyssey	73.5	Toyota Avalon	68.0
Acura TL	73.6	Lexus ES	69.1
Volvo V70	73.7	Honda Odyssey	70.2
Toyota Highlander	73.8	Toyota Tundra	70.7
Mitsubishi Outlander	73.9	Honda CR-V	71.2
Honda Pilot	74.9	Toyota Highlander	71.4
Dodge Neon	75.5	Acura TL	71.5
Subaru Forester	75.6	Subaru Forester	71.8
Honda Civic Hybrid	75.9	Nissan Frontier	71.9
Honda Accord	76.1	Acura TSX	72.6
Acura TSX	77.0	Subaru Legacy Outback	73.7
Pontiac Vibe	77.1	Subaru Impreza WRX	74.0
Subaru Legacy	77.1	Subaru Legacy	74.9
Lexus IS	77.6	Honda Pilot	74.9

71

Table 7 (Continued)
COMPARISON OF 2004 "RECOMMENDED" USED VEHICLE*
NADA RETAIL VALUES
(September 2007)

As % of Original M.S.R.P.		As % of 2007 M.S.R.P.†	
Lexus GX	78.3	Lexus RX	75.2
Jeep Liberty	78.6	Lexus GX	75.7
Nissan Altima	79.0	Pontiac Vibe	75.8
Toyota Sequoia	79.8	Honda Accord	76.0
Ford F-150 Heritage	80.0	Subaru Outback	76.0
Ford Ranger (4WD)	80.9	Honda Element	76.1
Acura RSX	81.8	Toyota Corolla	76.8
Toyota 4Runner	81.8	Toyota Camry	76.8
Infiniti G35 Sedan (AWD)	82.6	Toyota 4Runner	80.4
Infiniti FX	83.1	Toyota Matrix	81.0
Toyota Camry	83.1	Toyota RAV4	81.4
Lexus RX	83.3	Toyota Prius	82.5
Toyota Camry Solara	84.6	Scion xB	84.0
Toyota Corolla	85.5	Scion xA	84.9
Honda CR-V	85.7	Mazda 3	86.6
Scion xA	86.1	Subaru Impreza	88.0
Scion xB	86.9	Porsche 911	91.3
Honda Element	87.7	Toyota Tacoma	100.8
Subaru Impreza	88.5	Acura RSX	n.a.
Toyota Matrix	89.5	Buick Century	n.a.
Toyota Prius	91.5	Buick LeSabre	n.a.
Toyota RAV4	93.0	Buick Regal	n.a.
Mazda 3	93.7	Buick Rendezvous	n.a.
Nissan Frontier	94.0	Dodge Neon	n.a.
Porsche 911	96.4	Ford F-150 Heritage	n.a.
Toyota Echo	96.9	Ford Taurus	n.a.
Honda Civic	97.6	Infiniti I35	n.a.
Toyota Tundra	98.8	Mercury Sable	n.a.
Toyota Tacoma	116.5	Toyota Echo	n.a.

* From *Consumer Reports* list of "reliable used vehicles," April 2007. † Same or comparable new model. na Indicates no comparable model available..

Table 8
**COMPARISON OF 2005 "RECOMMENDED" USED VEHICLE*
NADA RETAIL VALUES**
(September 2007)

As % of Original M.S.R.P.		As % of 2007 M.S.R.P.†	
Buick Century	48.9	Lincoln Town Car	50.3
Buick LeSabre	52.2	Hyundai Accent	55.6
Ford Taurus	54.8	Volvo S80	60.4
Lincoln Town Car	57.1	Mazda B-Series (2WD)	62.0
Mercury Sable	57.2	Infiniti FX	64.0
Mazda B-Series (2WD)	62.9	Hyundai Sonata	64.3
Volvo S80	65.1	Hyundai Sante Fe	65.7
Buick Rendezvous (FWD)	65.1	Buick LaCrosse	68.3
Pontiac Grand Prix	66.3	Buick Rendezvous (FWD)	68.4
Hyundai Sonata	66.6	Volvo S60 (AWD)	68.8
Buick LaCrosse	67.0	Pontiac Grand Prix	69.3
Mazda MPV	68.2	Honda Accord Hybrid	69.6
Saab 9-2X	68.4	Toyota Tundra	70.5
Honda Accord Hybrid	69.8	Hyundai Elantra	70.5
Subaru Outback	71.8	Toyota Sequoia	70.6
Hyundai Sante Fe	73.3	Chevrolet Avalanche 1500	70.6
Honda S2000	74.4	Toyota Camry Solara	71.1
Lexus LX	74.8	Lexus LS	71.4
Chevrolet Avalanche 1500	75.1	Honda S2000	71.6
Hyundai Elantra	76.3	Lexus LX	71.9
Lexus SC	76.5	Nissan Altima	72.2
Mazda MX-5 Miata	77.8	Mazda MX-5 Miata	72.4
Lexus LS	78.3	Volvo S60 (FWD)	72.9
Subaru Impreza WRX	79.9	Honda Civic	73.6
Toyota Land Cruiser	80.7	Lexus SC	73.8
Toyota Highlander	82.0	Ford Explorer Sport Trac	73.9
Volvo S60 (FWD)	82.4	Honda Civic Hybrid	74.0
Volvo S60 (AWD)	82.7	Acura MDX	76.4
Pontiac Vibe	83.2	Toyota Land Cruiser	79.0
Acura MDX	83.3	Toyota Highlander	79.4
Hyundai Accent	83.4	Lexus ES	80.9
Honda Accord	83.7	Infiniti G35 Sedan	82.3
Ford Explorer Sport Trac	83.8	Acura TL	82.4
Acura TL	84.2	Subaru Forester	82.5
Lexus ES	84.7	Volvo XC70	83.1
Ford Ranger (2WD)	84.9	Acura TSX	83.1
Nissan Altima	85.0	Honda CR-V	83.3
Infiniti G35 Sedan	85.0	Toyota Camry	83.7
Honda Civic Hybrid	85.1	Nissan Murano	83.9
Honda Pilot	85.2	Pontiac Vibe	84.0
Subaru Forester	85.6	Lexus RX	84.7
Dodge Neon	86.1	Honda Accord	85.3
Acura TSX	86.5	Subaru Outback	85.3
Nissan Murano	86.7	Toyota Sienna	85.6
Volvo XC70	86.8	Honda Element	85.7
Subaru Baja	86.9	Honda Pilot	86.0

Table 8 (Continued)
COMPARISON OF 2005 "RECOMMENDED" USED VEHICLE*
NADA RETAIL VALUES
(September 2007)

As % of Original M.S.R.P.		As % of 2007 M.S.R.P.†	
Lexus GX	88.8	Toyota Corolla	86.6
Toyota Sienna	89.0	Subaru Impreza WRX	86.6
Toyota 4Runner	89.4	Lexus GX	87.2
Toyota Camry Solara	89.6	Toyota Prius	88.3
Subaru Legacy	90.2	Toyota Avalon	88.7
Toyota Avalon	90.5	Toyota 4Runner	88.9
Toyota Camry	90.5	Ford Ranger (2WD)	89.0
Acura RSX	91.4	Toyota RAV4	89.7
Toyota Sequoia	91.7	Scion xB	90.6
Infiniti FX	91.8	Scion xA	92.0
Lexus RX	91.9	Toyota Matrix	92.3
Scion xA	93.2	Subaru Legacy	92.3
Scion xB	93.8	BMW 3 Series	95.5
Toyota Prius	93.8	Mazda 3	98.7
Honda CR-V	95.2	Subaru Impreza	101.0
Toyota Corolla	95.6	Toyota Tacoma	109.9
Honda Element	96.8	Acura RSX	n.a.
Toyota Tundra	98.4	Buick Century	n.a.
Subaru Impreza	101.0	Buick LeSabre	n.a.
Toyota Matrix	101.3	Dodge Neon	n.a.
Toyota RAV4	101.3	Ford Taurus	n.a.
BMW 3 Series	105.6	Infiniti G35 Coupe	n.a.
Mazda 3	106.8	Mazda MPV	n.a.
Honda Civic	109.1	Mercury Sable	n.a.
Toyota Echo	110.3	Saab 9-2X	n.a.
Toyota Tacoma	116.1	Subaru Baja	n.a.
Infiniti G35 Coupe	n.a.	Toyota Echo	n.a.

* From *Consumer Reports* list of "reliable used vehicles," April 2007. † Same or comparable new model. na Indicates no comparable model available..

Table 9
COMPARISON OF 2006 "RECOMMENDED" USED VEHICLE* NADA RETAIL VALUES
(September 2007)

As % of Original M.S.R.P.		As % of 2007 M.S.R.P.†	
Buick Rendezvous (FWD)	70.7	Hyundai Sante Fe	73.1
Buick LaCrosse	73.7	Volvo S80	73.6
Volvo S80	75.8	Buick Rendezvous (FWD)	74.6
Honda Accord Hybrid	75.9	Buick LaCrosse	75.4
Chevrolet Avalanche 1500	76.5	Toyota Camry Solara	77.8
Subaru Outback	77.2	Honda Accord Hybrid	78.1
Acura TL	79.9	Toyota Tundra	79.7
Buick Lucerne	80.2	Buick Lucerne	81.9
Subaru B9 Tribeca	81.2	Toyota Sequoia	82.6
Hyundai Sante Fe	81.4	Subaru B9 Tribeca	83.1
Lexus LX	84.1	Lexus LX	83.6
Lincoln Zephyr	84.5	Mitsubishi Eclipse	83.7
Hyundai Azera	85.0	Infiniti M	84.3
Toyota Highlander Hybrid	86.1	Chevrolet Avalanche 1500	84.7
Volvo S60 (FWD)	87.2	Lexus LS	84.7
Mercury Milan	87.6	Mercury Milan	85.0
Subaru Impreza WRX	88.0	Ford Fusion	85.1
Honda Accord	89.1	Hyundai Azera	85.3
Mitsubishi Eclipse	89.6	Volvo S60 (FWD)	85.4
Nissan Altima (V6)	90.3	Hyundai Elantra	86.1
Hyundai Elantra	90.6	Nissan Altima (V6)	86.6
Ford Fusion	90.7	Honda Civic Hybrid	88.0
Honda Civic Hybrid	91.0	Honda Civic	89.0
Infiniti G35 Sedan	91.0	Infiniti G35 Sedan	89.9
Lexus LS	91.4	Toyota Camry	89.9
Toyota Highlander	91.7	Acura MDX	90.0
Acura TSX	91.9	Nissan Xterra	90.4
Subaru Forester	92.4	Toyota Highlander	90.4
Lexus RX Hybrid	92.6	Lexus ES	91.0
Infiniti M	93.7	Acura TSX	91.2
Lexus ES	94.3	Honda CR-V	91.5
Pontiac Vibe	94.6	Subaru Forester	91.5
Subaru Legacy	94.8	Nissan Frontier	92.1
Toyota Camry	95.2	Scion tC	92.4
Volvo V70 (FWD)	95.2	Pontiac Vibe	92.7
Acura MDX	97.0	Volvo V70 (FWD)	93.3
Toyota Camry Solara	97.4	Subaru Impreza WRX	93.7
Toyota Avalon	97.5	Subaru Outback	93.8
Toyota Prius	97.9	Honda Accord	95.7
Scion tC	98.1	Toyota Highlander Hybrid	95.9
Honda Pilot	99.2	Toyota Prius	95.9
Volvo XC70	99.4	Lexus RX	96.1
Lexus GX	99.7	Toyota Avalon	96.6
Nissan 350Z	101.0	Lexus RX Hybrid	97.1
Toyota Sienna	101.3	Volvo XC70	97.3
Toyota 4Runner	101.5	Lexus IS	97.9

75

Table 9 (Continued)
COMPARISON OF 2006 "RECOMMENDED" USED VEHICLE*
NADA RETAIL VALUES
(September 2007)

As % of Original M.S.R.P.		As % of 2007 M.S.R.P.†	
Scion xB	101.9	Toyota Corolla	98.1
Honda CR-V	102.5	Honda Element	98.2
Lexus RX	102.5	Honda Pilot	98.8
Nissan Xterra	104.7	Toyota Sienna	99.0
Toyota Corolla	105.8	Lexus GX	99.5
Toyota Sequoia	106.2	Scion xB	100.0
Toyota RAV4	108.0	Subaru Legacy	100.4
Nissan Frontier	108.6	Toyota 4Runner	101.5
Honda Element	109.0	Toyota Matrix	102.8
Toyota Tundra	110.0	Toyota RAV4	104.6
Toyota Matrix	110.3	Mazda 3	110.5
Lexus IS	111.9	Subaru Impreza	115.0
Subaru Impreza	113.1	Acura TL	115.4
Mazda 3	119.2	Toyota Tacoma	122.9
Honda Civic	120.9	Cadillac DTS	73.4
Toyota Tacoma	126.4	Lincoln Zephyr	n.a.
Cadillac DTS	79.4	Nissan 350Z	n.a.

* From *Consumer Reports* list of "reliable used vehicles," April 2007. † Same or comparable new model. na Indicates no comparable model available..

V.

SHOULD YOU BUY OR LEASE?

MANY salesmen, whether they are trying to sell or lease a car, rely on the amount of the monthly payment as a means of persuading people that they can "afford" to buy (or lease) a particular car. As we point out in Chapter IX, monthly payment amounts and actual ownership costs are not the same. **From an economic viewpoint, in most situations you should pay cash for a car and keep running it as long as possible.** What is "affordable" ought to be determined with reference to an individual's and family's overall financial plans, and car costs ought to be considered from the perspective of both short-term and long-term outlays rather than quick figuring in the showroom to reduce the monthly payments.*

Over the last 15 years or so, leasing has grown in popularity among car shoppers. Its popularity waxes and wanes depending on how attractive the lease deals are. In recent years they have become less generous. One reason is that the "residual values" of leased cars (the value of the vehicle when the lease ends) has not been as high as car makers anticipated, partly because a glut of used cars has driven down used-car prices. To make up for these lower-than-expected values, car makers have raised the monthly payments and up-front fees on new leases.

A lease is equivalent to borrowing money to purchase a car with a guarantee to sell it back at the end of a term. When you lease a car, you are essentially paying for only the portion of the car's worth that you "use"—that is, the expected depreciation—plus a lease fee to the lease company. In most instances, you will be responsible for all maintenance on the vehicle, including the maintenance required to maintain warranty coverage.

The primary advantages of leasing are that your monthly payments may be lower than they would be if you purchased the car on credit, and you may be able to drive a better car than you could afford to buy. The downside, of course, is that you do not own the car. The monthly payments are lower because at the end of the lease period, typically two to four years, you have

---

* Our book "Sensible Budgeting with the Rubber Budget Account Book" is a helpful guide to family budgeting. It can be ordered at www.aier.org/bookstore.

no equity interest in the car. It is the dealer who owns the car, not you, and any resale value accrues to the dealer instead of you.

Another benefit of leasing is that you may not have to commit a substantial amount of cash up front. Because of the time value of money, it is beneficial not to have to commit cash, whether for a down payment or for the entire purchase price of a car. That is, the down payment used to buy a car on credit could be invested in an interest-bearing account if you lease a car instead. Looked at another way, the lease contract allows you to forgo the trouble of saving for several months to put together a down payment, or for the several years it may take to accumulate the entire price of a car. Either way, the value of this consideration varies with the rate of interest you expect to earn on your savings. Its value also depends on the terms of the lease agreement. Many dealers require that you make a large up-front payment, comparable to a down payment, when you lease a car.

A disadvantage of leasing is that if you buy a car on credit instead of leasing it, the interest portion of your loan payments may be deductible from income for tax purposes. The 1986 tax reform phased out the interest-cost deductions for car loans and other consumer debt, but interest paid on home equity loans still is deductible. Thus, a homeowner who takes out a home equity loan to finance the purchase of a car can still benefit from the interest deduction—something he cannot do if he leases the car. However, this deduction is available only to homeowners who itemize their tax returns. In addition, borrowers should realize that a home equity loan is a loan against the value of their house, even if the funds are used to buy a car. In the event they fail to repay the loan, it is the house, not the car, which may be seized by creditors.

Aside from the tax considerations, there are other factors that can increase the cost of leasing. For example, most leases impose mileage restrictions (usually 10,000 to 15,000 miles per year) and fees for excess mileage (10 to 25 cents per additional mile). It may be more expensive to insure a leased vehicle because leasing companies require a minimum amount of insurance coverage (see below). As noted, some require a large up-front payment that is essentially a down payment (although a portion of it may be refundable). Most contracts carry hefty penalties for early termination and charges for excess wear and tear. In addition, you may wish to consider "gap insurance" to cover the difference—sometimes thousands of dollars—between what you owe on the lease and what the car is worth, should the car be stolen or totaled in an accident. These outright or contingent charges can wipe out most, if not all, of the benefits of leasing.

Understanding a Lease

Although they are improving, many leasing arrangements are quite complex and confusing to many consumers. Before signing a lease it is important to make sure you fully understand the document you are signing. Unscrupulous dealers will try to hide important information from you. There are several guides and "worksheets" available to help compare leasing deals. The Federal Reserve offers a free brochure "Keys to Vehicle Leasing." You can get a copy by phoning (202) 452-3244(5), by visiting their website at www.federalreserve.gov/pubs/leasing, or by writing to Publications Fulfillment, Board of Governors of the Federal Reserve Board, Mail Stop 127, Washington, D.C., 20551.

Federal Reserve Regulation M, which covers the consumer leasing provisions of the Truth in Lending Act, and some state laws may provide you with additional consumer rights not covered in your lease agreement. For information on these laws, contact your state's consumer protection agency or Attorney General's office. The Federal Trade Commission also publishes a helpful brochure, "Understanding Vehicle Financing." For a free copy, visit www.ftc.gov/bcp/edu/pubs/consumer/autos/aut04.shtm or call 1-877-FTC-HELP (382-4357).

There are two types of leases: a "closed-end" and an "open-end." With a closed-end lease, you are not responsible for the value of the car at the end of the lease. However, because the dealer is taking the risk as to what the car will be worth at the end of the lease agreement, the monthly payments on a closed-end lease are usually higher than in an open-end lease. Note that even if you "walk away," you are usually responsible for certain end-of-lease charges, such as excess mileage, wear and tear, and the cost of prepping the vehicle for resale.

With an open-end lease, you may have lower monthly payments, but you take on the risk that the car may not be worth the amount specified in the lease contract—often called the estimated residual value or estimated resale value. In such cases, you are responsible for paying the difference if the actual resale value is less than the estimated resale value. (Conversely, your lease agreement may provide for a refund of any excess if the realized value is greater than the residual value.) If you believe the amount owed at the end of the lease term is unreasonable and refuse to pay, the lessor or assignee may attempt to prove that the residual value was reasonable when it was set at the beginning of the lease. However, if you cannot reach a settlement with the lessor or assignee, you cannot be forced to pay the excess amount unless the lessor or assignee brings a successful court ac-

Box 1
SEGREGATED DISCLOSURES

Date _____

Lessor(s) _____ Lessee(s) _____

Amount Due at Lease Signing or Delivery (Itemized below)* $ _____	Monthly Payments Your first monthly payment of $ _____ is due on _____, followed by _____ payments of $ _____ due on the _____ of each month. The total of your monthly payments is $ _____.	Other Charges (not part of your monthly payment) Disposition fee (if you do not purchase the vehicle) $ _____ Total $ _____	Total of Payments (The amount you will have paid by the end of the lease) $ _____

* Itemization of Amount Due at Lease Signing or Delivery

Amount Due at Lease Signing or Delivery:

Capitalized cost reduction $ _____
First monthly payment   _____
Refundable security deposit   _____
Title fees   _____
Registration fees   _____
                        Total $ _____

How the Amount Due at Lease Signing or Delivery will be paid:

Net trade-in allowance $ _____
Rebates and noncash credits _____
Amount to be paid in cash   _____

                        Total $ _____

Your monthly payment is determined as shown below:

Gross capitalized cost. The agreed upon value of the vehicle ($ _____) and any items you pay over the lease term (such as service contracts, insurance, and any outstanding prior credit or lease balance) .... $ _____

If you want an itemization of this amount, please check this box. ☐

Capitalized cost reduction. The amount of any net trade-in allowance, rebate, noncash credit, or cash you pay that reduces the gross capitalized cost .... − _____
Adjusted capitalized cost. The amount used in calculating your base monthly payment .... = _____
Residual value. The value of the vehicle at the end of the lease used in calculating your base monthly payment .... − _____
Depreciation and any amortized amounts. The amount charged for the vehicle's decline in value through normal use and for other items paid over the lease term .... = _____
Rent charge. The amount charged in addition to the depreciation and any amortized amounts .... + _____
Total of base monthly payments. The depreciation and any amortized amounts plus the rent charge .... = _____
Lease payments. The number of payments in your lease .... ÷ _____
Base monthly payment .... = _____
Monthly sales/use tax .... + _____

Total monthly payment .... =$ _____

Early Termination. You may have to pay a substantial charge if you end this lease early. <u>The charge may be up to several thousand dollars.</u> The actual charge will depend on when the lease is terminated. The earlier you end the lease, the greater this charge is likely to be.

Excessive Wear and Use. You may be charged for excessive wear based on our standards for normal use [and for mileage in excess of _____ miles per year at the rate of _____ per mile].

Purchase Option at End of Lease Term. [You have an option to purchase the vehicle at the end of the lease term for $ _____ [and a purchase option fee of $ _____].] [You do not have an option to purchase the vehicle at the end of the lease term.]

Other Important Terms. See your lease documents for additional information on early termination, purchase options and maintenance responsibilities, warranties, late and default charges, insurance, and any security interest, if applicable.

tion and pays your reasonable attorney's fees. (Assuming you have met the mileage and wear standards, the residual value is considered unreasonable if it exceeds the realized value by more than three times the base monthly payment, sometimes called the "three-payment rule.")

Carmakers have sometimes lost a great deal of money on lease deals, by overestimating what vehicles would be worth at the end of the lease. Both a glut of late-model used vehicles and generous sales incentives on new cars have depressed used-car prices during the past couple of years. To stem these "residual losses," carmakers have made new leases less generous. For example, they have lowered their estimates of how much they think vehicles will be worth at the end of the lease, and raised monthly lease payments to

Box 2
NONSEGREGATED DISCLOSURES

[The following provisions are the nonsegregated disclosures required under Regulation M.]

Description of Leased Property				
Year	Make	Model	Body Style	Vehicle ID #

Official Fees and Taxes. The total amount you will pay for official and license fees, registration, title, and taxes over the term of your lease, whether included with your monthly payments or assessed otherwise: $ _____ .

Insurance. The following types and amounts of insurance will be acquired in connection with this lease: _____

_____ We (lessor) will provide the insurance coverage quoted above for a total premium cost of $ _____ .

_____ You (lessee) agree to provide insurance coverage in the amount and types indicated above.

Standards for Wear and Use. The following standards are applicable for determining unreasonable or excess wear and use of the leased vehicle: _____

Maintenance.
[You are responsible for the following maintenance and servicing of the leased vehicle:
_____].

[We are responsible for the following maintenance and servicing of the leased vehicle:
_____].

Warranties. The leased vehicle is subject to the following express warranties: _____

Early Termination and Default. (a) You may terminate this lease before the end of the lease term under the following conditions: _____

The charge for such early termination is: _____

(b) We may terminate this lease before the end of the lease term under the following conditions: _____

Upon such termination we shall be entitled to the following charge(s) for: _____

(c) To the extent these charges take into account the value of the vehicle at termination, if you disagree with the value we assign to the vehicle, you may obtain, at your own expense, from an independent third party agreeable to both of us, a professional appraisal of the _____ value of the leased vehicle which could be realized at sale. The appraised value shall then be used as the actual value.

Security Interest. We reserve a security interest of the following type in the property listed below to secure performance of your obligations under this lease: _____

Late Payments. The charge for late payments is: _____

Option to Purchase Leased Property Prior to the End of the Lease. [You have an option to purchase the leased vehicle prior to the end of the term. The price will be [$ _____ /[the method of determining the price].] [You do not have an option to purchase the leased vehicle.]

make up for that reduction in expected resale value.

As with buying a new car, you should always shop around. Negotiate *all* lease terms, including the price of the vehicle, residual value, mileage allowance, etc. Ask questions, nail down the details, read the fine print, and most importantly—get all terms in writing.

Under the Consumer Leasing Act, a vehicle lessor must provide the lessee (i.e., consumer) with certain information (if the lease is for $25,000 or less). Some of the information, called "segregated disclosures," must appear on a form like the one in Box 1 on page 80. Other information that must be provided, called "nonsegregated information," shown in Box 2 on page 81, will not necessarily appear on a form or in one place on the lease. These boxes contain information you should know before signing a lease, and make it easier to compare deals.

The amount you will have paid by the end of the lease is the sum of the amount due at lease signing or delivery, the total of your monthly payments, and other charges that are not part of your monthly payment, such as a disposition fee (a fee that helps cover the cost of selling the car at the end of the lease). This figure does not include refundable amounts such as a security deposit or amounts that may be due if you end the lease early or exceed wear or mileage limits.

The monthly payment is the sum of the following three items: the monthly depreciation fee, the monthly rent charge or lease fee, and sales tax. To arrive at the monthly depreciation fee and monthly finance charge, you must begin with the capitalized cost and work toward the net capitalized cost. The price of the car is referred to as the "capitalized cost." To this price you add optional service contracts, insurance, and any other fees to get the "gross capitalized cost" of the car. Insist that the lessor itemize the gross capitalized cost so you know what this total includes.

From the gross capitalized cost, you deduct your down payment, trade-in allowance, and rebates (if any), to get the "net capitalized cost" of the car. The more you can lower the capitalized cost of the car, the lower your monthly payments will be. The fees you deduct from the gross capitalized cost are called "capitalized cost reductions." When negotiating a lease, if you wish, you can pay an up-front capitalized-cost reduction. This is similar to a down payment on a car and it will reduce the amount that you finance over the length of the lease, thus lowering your monthly lease payment. However, this will minimize one of the attractive features of a lease, which is a low initial cost.

Depreciation is the difference between the net capitalized cost and the value of the car at the end of lease or "residual value." Residual value is usually expressed as a percentage of the M.S.R.P. Since you pay for the depreciation of the car, the higher the residual value, the less depreciation you have to pay for. To find the monthly depreciation fee, simply divide the amount of depreciation by the lease term.

A large portion of your monthly payment—the lease fee—is for financing the car while you drive it. The lease fee, which is calculated differently than the interest on a loan, is arrived at using the following formula: (net capitalized cost plus residual value) times the "money factor." The "money factor" is often expressed as a six-digit decimal number. To figure out an approximate interest rate that you can compare to other car loans, multiply the money factor by 2400. For example, a money factor of .002917 would be equivalent to about a 7.0 percent loan. Similar to an auto loan, the lower the money factor the lower your monthly payment.

The monthly sales tax (based on where you live, not where the vehicle is purchased) is computed by adding the monthly depreciation and lease fees and then multiplying by your state's tax rate. This does not apply in Alaska, New Hampshire and Oregon. Note that although most states tax only your monthly depreciation, some apply the sales tax to the full amount of the car (for example in Illinois and Texas)—even though you are not buying the car. Most states also tax the lease fee. These taxes greatly reduce the incentive to lease in such states; as does the policy in states like New York which require tax payments up-front on the entire sum of lease payments.

Given the monthly payment, it is now possible to calculate the amount due at signing or delivery, and how that amount will be paid. Again, insist on an itemization. The amount due at signing may include some or all of the following: capitalized cost reduction, the first monthly payment, a security deposit, a destination charge, an acquisition fee, and title and registration fees. Some combination of trade-in allowance, rebates, and cash is generally used to pay the amount due.

The "nonsegregated disclosures" provide information on early termination, purchase options and maintenance responsibilities, warranties, late and default charges, insurance, and security interest (if applicable). Unfortunately, these items do not necessarily appear on a form or in one place in the lease. Nonetheless, they are of critical importance. For example, to avoid later disputes, be sure you understand the standards for wear and use, and what is considered excess. Failure to consider these details could result in large end-of-lease costs. Needless to say, this information should be documented in writing.

Comparing Financing Methods

Deciding whether to buy a car outright, to buy on credit, or to lease is not simple. Table 10 gives a hypothetical illustration of the relative costs of these three options over a four-year period. In our illustration we assume that the cash price is $25,000, that the down payment on the credit purchase is 20 percent of the total price ($5,000), and that the interest rate is 7.0 percent on a loan used to finance the car. We assume that if the buyer took out a home equity loan to finance his purchase he would be subject to a combined Federal and state effective income tax rate of 25 percent. For the lease, we assume a monthly payment amount that is based on amortizing the difference between the car's current value and its expected resale value. We also have assumed that the lessee is required to post a refundable security deposit equal to one monthly payment. Finally, we assume that the car's dollar value depreciates 70 percent over four years.

If we ignore the time value of money, the simple net cost of the car

Table 10
**ILLUSTRATED SIMPLE AND DISCOUNTED
4-YEAR COST OF A $25,000 AUTOMOBILE
BY METHOD OF PAYMENT**

Outlays	*Cash*	*Loan*	*Lease*
1. Initial payment/security deposit	$25,000	$ 5,000	$ 419
2. Monthly payment	0	$479	$419
× 48 months	0	22,992	20,112
3. Total Outlays (line 1 + line 2)	$25,000	$27,992	$20,531
Receipts			
4. Resale value/security deposit	$7,500	$7,500	$ 419
5. Tax deductions	0	747	0
6. Total Receipts (line 4 + line 5)	$7,500	$8,247	$ 419
Net Cost			
7. Simple (line 3 − line 6)	$17,500	$19,745	$20,112
8. Discounted at 3%	18,353	19,249	18,948
9. Discounted at 9%	19,725	18,325	16,953

(line 7 in the table) is the difference between total outlays (line 3) and total receipts (line 6). The amounts shown suggest that leasing is the most costly method of payment. The disadvantage of leasing becomes less clear, however, when we acknowledge the time value of money. Lines 8 and 9 show the "discounted" net cost of each of the three methods of payment. These calculations take into account the idea that future outlays are less burdensome than present outlays and future receipts are less valuable than present receipts. As the discount rate (the expected interest rate on savings accounts or similar investments) rises, future outlays and receipts are worth less while "up-front" costs weigh more heavily. In our illustration, for example, when the discount rate is three percent, leasing becomes a better option than purchasing on credit, and when the discount rate rises as high as nine percent, leasing becomes the most attractive option.

This illustration underscores how important it is to factor the time value of money into a comparison of payment methods. A comparison of the "simple net costs" of payment methods becomes more and more misleading as interest rates rise. Depending on the interest-rate differential between one's savings account and one's loan account, in some circumstances buying a car on credit actually may be the least costly method of purchasing a car even if you have the savings to pay cash for it. If your interest-rate return on a long-term investment is higher than the interest that you would have to pay on money borrowed to purchase the car (say, if the dealer offers a below-market loan rate as a sales incentive), you are better off borrowing the money and allowing your savings to accumulate interest at the higher rate.

Before making the decision to lease, you should make your own comparison of the costs and benefits of buying as opposed to leasing. You can obtain information on monthly payments, the security deposit, the down payment, and the expected resale value of the car from your bank and your car dealer. (As with buying a car, you should comparison shop to find the best lease.) Use these figures to construct a table similar to Table 10, using as a discount rate an estimate of how much you can earn on your savings account, money-market account, or other reasonably safe and liquid investments. In most cases, you will be better off to purchase the car with cash.

VI.

SAFETY RECALLS AND LEMON LAWS

THE National Highway Traffic Safety Administration (NHTSA) maintains many databases that provide information on vehicle safety recalls, technical service bulletins, defect investigations, consumer complaints, safety studies and more. You can access these databases at the NHTSA web site, www.nhtsa.gov. You can also get information on safety recalls, and report safety problems with vehicles, by calling NHTSA's toll-free hotline, 1-888-327-4236. The website is highly recommended for anyone contemplating the purchase of a used car. Even if you are buying a new car, reading about the history of older models gives you valuable insights into which models are most likely to be trouble-free.

At NHTSA's website, the "recalls" search engine lets you search the NHTSA Recall Campaigns database by year, make, or model. Recall information is also available for equipment, child-safety seats, and tires. Each report includes a brief summary outlining the problem, its safety implications, and a course of action. (The "defect investigations" link contains information on active defect investigations, defect petitions, and recall petitions.)

For instance, GM has recalled over 10,000 Chevrolet Express and GMC Savanna vans from the 2007 model year due to problems with rear brakes sticking, which could increase stopping distances. Additionally, Toyota has recalled over 30,000 Echo and Prius passenger vehicles from model years 2001-2002 due to problems with the crankshaft position sensor that could cause the engine to stall while driving.

At the "complaints" section of NHTSA's website, you can look up a particular vehicle and read complaints submitted by customers, dealers, and mechanics. Caution is in order: These complaints are not subject to any verification, and it is not clear how representative they are of the typical car owner's experience. Nonetheless, they are well worth checking. They can be quite eye-opening and even downright alarming. Indeed, after reading about cars suddenly accelerating "on their own," engines shutting down while the car is in motion, loose wires causing fires, airbags failing to deploy, wheels falling off, and sunroofs exploding, you may be tempted to give up driving altogether.

STATE CONSUMER PROTECTION AGENCIES

Alabama .... Consumer Affairs Section, Office of Atty. Gen., www.ago.state.al.us .... (800) 392-5658
Alaska .... Consumer Protection Unit, Office of Atty. Gen., www.law.state.ak.us .... (907) 269-5100
Arizona .... Consumer Protection Section, Office of Atty. Gen., www.ag.state.az.us .... (800) 352-8431
Arkansas .... Consumer Protection Division, Office of Atty. Gen., www.ag.state.ar.us .... (800) 482-8982
California .... Department of Consumer Affairs, www.dca.ca.gov .... (800) 952-5210

Colorado .... Consumer Protection Division, Office of Atty. Gen., www.ago.state.co.us .... (800) 222-4444
Connecticut .... Department of Consumer Protection, www.ct.gov/dcp .... (860) 713-6050
Delaware .... Fraud and Consumer Protection Division, Office of Atty. Gen., www.attorneygeneral.delaware.gov .... (800) 220-5424
Dist.of Columbia .. Consumer Protection Section, 441 4th St., NW, Suite 450 North, Washington, DC 20001, www.oag.dc.gov .... (202) 442-4400
Florida .... Economic Crimes Division, Office of Atty. Gen., www.myfloridalegal.com .... (866) 966-7226

Georgia .... Governor's Office of Consumer Affairs, www.consumer.georgia.gov .... (800) 869-1123
Hawaii .... Office of Consumer Protection, www.state.hi.us/dlcca/ .... (808) 587-3222
Idaho .... Consumer Protection Unit, Office of Atty. Gen., www2.state.id.us/ag .... (800) 432-3545
Illinois .... Consumer Protection Division, Office of Atty. Gen., www.ag.state.il.us .... (800) 386-5438
Indiana .... Consumer Protection Division, Office of Atty. Gen., www.indianaconsumer.com .... (800) 382-5516
Iowa .... Consumer Protection Division, Office of Atty. Gen., www.IowaAttorneyGeneral.org .... (888) 777-4590

Kansas .... Consumer Protection Division, Office of Atty. Gen., www.ksag.org .... (800) 432-2310
Kentucky .... Consumer Protection Division, Office of Atty. Gen., www.ag.ky.gov/consumer .... (888) 432-9257
Louisiana .... Consumer Protection Section, Office of Atty. Gen., www.ag.state.la.us .... (800) 351-4889
Maine .... Consumer Protection Division, Office of Atty. Gen., www.maine.gov/ag .... (800) 461-2131
Maryland .... Consumer Protection Division, Office of Atty. Gen., www.oag.state.md.us/consumer .... (888) 743-0023

Massachusetts ..... Office of Consumer Affairs & Business Regulation, www.mass.gov/consumer .... (888) 283-3757
Michigan .... Consumer Protection Division, Office of Atty. Gen., www.michigan.gov/ag .... (517) 335-0855
Minnesota .... Consumer Services Division, Office of Atty. Gen., www.ag.state.mn.us/consumer .... (800) 657-3787
Mississippi .... Consumer Protection Division, Office of Atty. Gen.,www.ago.state.ms.us .... (800) 281-4418

Missouri	Consumer Protection Division, Office of Atty. Gen., www.ago.mo.gov/Consumer-Protection.htm	(800) 392-8222
Montana	Consumer Protection Office, www.doj.mt.gov/consumer/	(800) 481-6896
Nebraska	Consumer Protection Division, Office of Atty. Gen., www.ago.state.ne.us	(800) 727-6432
Nevada	Consumer Affairs Division, www.fyiconsumer.org	(800) 326-5202
New Hampshire	Consumer Protection Bureau, Office of Atty. Gen., www.doj.nh.gov/consumer/index.html	(888) 468-4454
New Jersey	Division of Consumer Affairs, www.state.nj.us/lps/ca	(800) 242-5846
New Mexico	Consumer Protection Division, Office of the Atty. Gen., www.nmago.state.nm.us/divs/cons/cons.htm	(800) 678-1508
New York	Consumer Protection Board, www.consumer.state.ny.us	(800) 697-1220
North Carolina	Consumer Protection Division, Office of Atty. Gen., www.ncdoj.com	(877) 566-7226
North Dakota	Consumer Protection & Antitrust Division, Office of Atty. Gen., www.ag.state.nd.us	(800) 472-2600
Ohio	Consumer Protection Section, Office of Atty. Gen., www.ag.state.oh.us	(877) 244-6446
Oklahoma	Consumer Protection Unit, Office of Atty. Gen., www.oag.state.ok.us	(405) 521-3921
Oregon	Financial Fraud / Consumer Protection Section, Dept. of Justice, www.doj.state.or.us	(877) 877-9392
Pennsylvania	Bureau of Consumer Protection, Office of Atty. Gen., www.attorneygeneral.gov	(800) 441-2555
Rhode Island	Consumer Protection Unit, Dept. of the Atty. Gen., www.riag.state.ri.us/civil	(401) 274-4400
South Carolina	Dept. of Consumer Affairs, www.scconsumer.gov	(800) 922-1594
South Dakota	Division of Consumer Protection, www.state.sd.us/attorney	(800) 300-1986
Tennessee	Division of Consumer Affairs, www.state.tn.us/consumer	(800) 342-8385
Texas	Consumer Protection Division, Office of Atty. Gen., www.oag.state.tx.us	(800) 621-0508
Utah	Division of Consumer Protection, www.consumerprotection.utah.gov	(800) 721-7233
Vermont	Consumer Protection Unit, Office of Atty. Gen., www.atg.state.vt.us	(800) 649-2424
Virginia	Consumer Asstance, Office of the Attorney General, www.vaag.com/consumer	(804) 786-2071
Washington	Consumer Resource Center, Office of the Atty. Gen., www.atg.wa.gov	(800) 551-4636
West Virginia	Consumer Protection & Antitrust Division, Office of the Atty. Gen., www.wvago.gov	(800) 368-8808
Wisconsin	Dept. of Agriculture, Trade, and Consumer Protection, www.datcp.state.wi.us	(800) 422-7128
Wyoming	Consumer Protection Unit, Office of the Atty. Gen., http://attorneygeneral.state.wy.us	(800) 438-5799

The site also offers information on "technical service bulletins" (TSBs). These are put out by manufacturers to help automotive technicians fix difficult-to-diagnose problems such as rough idles, intermittent stalls, hard starts, etc. In general, the more problems a vehicle has, the more TSBs it has. Thus, the number of TSBs issued for a particular model of vehicle may be some indication of its mechanical soundness. For example, a recent review of the NHTSA database revealed that, as of September 2007, the 2005 GMC Envoy, a *Consumer Reports* "used car to avoid," had a total of 171 TSBs. In contrast, the 2005 Honda Element, a *Consumer Reports* "reliable used car," had only 28.

Lemon Laws

All states have enacted lemon laws designed to protect consumers in the event that a new car is seriously defective and the dealer is unable, or unwilling, to correct the problem. In general, to qualify as a lemon, a car must have a major problem that the manufacturer (not the dealer) has failed to repair after four attempts or must have been garaged for repairs for 30 cumulative days during the manufacturer's or dealer's warranty period. If a car qualifies as a lemon, the buyer is entitled to a refund of the purchase price of the vehicle, as well as reimbursement for other costs such as taxes and registration.

Most state statutes contain more stringent provisions than the Magnuson-Moss Warranty Act, a Federal statute that prohibits the exclusion of *implied* warranties on the purchase of consumer goods. State consumer protection offices (see listing on pages 88-89) can provide you with information about the specific warranty rights that car buyers have in each state. The Better Business Bureau also provides this information online at www.lemonlaw.bbb.org. Many of the state statutes, which do not preempt the Magnuson-Moss Act, have provisions that require complainants to enter an arbitration procedure before they resort to legal remedies in the state courts.

If you think you have a lemon, the most important evidence in your favor will be the documentation that you provide indicating that you informed the dealer of the problem, that he acknowledged the problem (by writing it on a repair order), and that he repeatedly failed to fix it. **Keep all repair records.**

Always test drive the car you have purchased before you accept it or hand over any cash. If you notice any defects, do not take delivery. Rather, require that the dealer repair them *before* the final sale is completed. Do not allow him to convince you that the problem is only a small one and that he will repair it when you return for routine service. The problem may be small—but it may not be. Once you accept the car and pay the dealer the full price, his incentive to make the repair is greatly reduced. If the problem does prove to be serious, then you will have to resort to the procedures prescribed by various state laws for lemons.

VII.

HOW TO USE THE *N.A.D.A. OFFICIAL USED CAR GUIDE**

THE values of used automobiles are recorded in the *N.A.D.A. Official Used Car Guide* and their Consumer Edition is available at the N.A.D.A. website, www.nadaguides.com. These values are used in most auto markets as a basis for negotiating the terms of sale of used cars. However, the book value listed in the *N.A.D.A. Guide* may differ substantially—either higher or lower—from the actual dollar value of the vehicle. Some salespersons may try to manipulate the amounts listed in the *Guide*. It is therefore in your interest to be familiar with its contents and with the procedures involved in pricing used automobiles.

In many cases, the listed book value of a car may be substantially higher than its actual dollar value. The values listed in the *N.A.D.A. Official Used Car Guide* assume that a car is clean. That is, those amounts assume that a vehicle has been maintained according to the manufacturer's specifications and that its condition reflects only the deterioration to be expected from normal wear and tear for a car of its vintage. A poorly maintained automobile, whether because of mechanical defects or cosmetic deterioration (say, rust) will be valued lower than the listed book value. In determining the price he is willing to offer on a trade-in, a dealer must deduct any amount that is required to recondition the car for resale from the amount listed in the *N.A.D.A. Guide*. On the other hand, an exceptionally well-maintained car ought to bring a price somewhat higher than the listed book value.

A brief description of the value categories listed in the *N.A.D.A. Guide* may save used car buyers and sellers from confusion and disappointment when it comes time to haggle over price.

---

* Your bank, credit union, or other lending institution will have a copy of the current *N.A.D.A. Official Used Car Guide*, which lists values of cars for years 2000-2007. Subscriptions to the *N.A.D.A. Official Used Car Guide* (12 issues per year) are obtainable for $70 per subscription from NADA Analytical Services Group, 8400 Wesstpark Drive, McLean, VA 22102-9985. Phone: 800-544-6267. www.nadaguides.com/priceguides. There are ten regional classifications for the *N.A.D.A. Guide*: New England (ME, MA, NH, RI, VT); Eastern (CT, DE, DC, MD, NJ, NY, PA, TN, VA, WV); Central (IL, IN, KY, MI, MO, OH, WI); Southeastern (AL, FL, GA, MS, NC, SC); Southwestern (AR, LA, OK, TX); Midwest (IA, KS, MN, NE, ND, SD); Desert Southwest (AZ, NV); Pacific Northwest (AK, ID, WA, OR, UT); Mountain (CO, MT, NM, WY); and California (CA, HI).

Four columns list amounts that relate in some way to the dollar value of a particular vehicle: (1) *Trade-In* (N.A.D.A.'s trade-in value), (2) *M.S.R.P.* (manufacturer's suggested retail price), (3) *Loan* (average amount of loan a bank is willing to lend for the purchase of the car), and (4) *Retail* (N.A.D.A.'s Retail Value).

Each of these categories describes a different measure. The retail value (the column at the far right-hand side of each page in the *N.A.D.A. Guide*) most nearly approximates the amount a car in clean condition will sell for on the retail market. According to N.A.D.A., "an exceptionally clean vehicle or one that bears a guarantee, warranty, or manufacturer certification should bring a premium price."

Do not confuse the average retail amount with the amount listed under the heading *Trade-In* at the far left-hand side of each page in the *N.A.D.A. Guide*. Some salespeople may point to the *Trade-In* figure as representing your car's potential retail value. It is *not*.

Thus, the term trade-in is improperly applied when used to describe the amounts in the column. The latter amount may have been higher or lower. In any event, the amounts listed under the *Trade-In* column reflect several adjustments from the average retail values listed in the right-hand column of the *N.A.D.A. Guide*: *e.g.*, the dealer profit margin, deduction of rehabilitation costs, etc. The important point is that the amount listed under *Trade-In* almost always will be *lower* than the actual *retail* value of your car, and your bargaining position should be based on retail value.

However, frequently there are adjustments to retail dollar values listed in the *N.A.D.A. Guide*. If your car needs mechanical repairs or body work done, then the cost of that work must be deducted from the retail value of the car. In most cases, and contrary to popular wisdom that dictates a car is ready to trade in when it starts to have trouble, **it is a fallacy to believe that substantial savings will be achieved by trading in a car when it develops problems that will be costly to repair.** The fact is, you will pay these repair costs anyhow as a deduction from the book value of the car.

Dealers often allow a $500, $1,000, or even $3,000 trade-in value even on junk cars. This allowance often does not reflect the actual value of your trade-in, but represents either an inflated new car price or reduced dealer profit on the new car. Even a vehicle with considerable book value may be economically worthless to a dealer if it needs costly repair work. One way or another this fact will be reflected in the final package that the dealer is willing to accept. When that is the case, and your present auto is still *safely operable*, you are better off financially to run it into the ground rather than to trade it in before its useful life has ended.

The farther a car has been driven, the less its remaining useful life, and, thus, the less its dollar value. A high mileage table in the *N.A.D.A. Guide* lists amounts to be deducted for specified mileage ranges for different cars. However, N.A.D.A. appraisal practices require that the high mileage deduction not exceed 40 percent of average trade-in value.

Although you can expect most salesmen to pay careful attention to this high mileage deduction, they are apt to be far less observant of a related requirement that adds to the value of some used vehicles: namely, an *added premium* for low mileage. The *N.A.D.A. Guide* also includes a "low-mileage table" that lists amounts that should be *added* to the retail value for specified mileage ranges and models. The addition can be substantial. For example, a 2002 Honda Accord LX Sedan (N.A.D.A. mileage category "Class II") driven between 25,001 and 30,000 miles as of April 2007 should be valued at $1,500 more than the listed retail value of $11,100. Note that N.A.D.A. appraisal practices limit the low mileage premium to no more than 50 percent of average trade-in value. The accompanying table lists the "normal" mileage ranges for automobile model years 2000-2007, as of mid-2007. Mileage higher than shown requires a high mileage deduction; while mileage that is lower than shown in the table requires that a specified amount be added to the car's listed value.

Model Year	Normal Mileage Range
2000	90,001-100,000
2001	80,001-90,000
2002	70,001-75,000
2003	55,001–60,000
2004	45,001–50,000
2005	30,001–35,000
2006	20,001–25,000
2007	7,501–15,000

If your present vehicle is approaching the upper limits of the low mileage (anything less than the lower figures in the table) or normal mileage ranges, and if it will cause no inconvenience (say, if you have a second car), then you might save several hundred dollars in retained book value simply by restricting driving so as not to exceed the N.A.D.A. mileage range before the car is traded in.

A publisher's preface in the *N.A.D.A. Guide* asserts that "optional equipment has little or no value on older vehicles." This printed statement could be a potent tool in the hands of a salesman trying to place you in a disadvantageous bargaining position, especially if your present car is loaded with high-priced options.

In fact, luxury options can add value to a used vehicle. This is acknowledged in the retail column of the *N.A.D.A. Guide*. Amounts are added to the listed retail value of a car for a variety of options, including aluminum/alloy wheels, leather seats, sunroof, premium stereo systems, etc. It is in your interest to find out the listed value, if any, of the options on your present car, and to present that list to sales personnel who may have been led to believe and trained to say—even in all honesty—that they are worthless.

The *Loan* column in the *N.A.D.A. Guide*, which is used by dealers to determine how large a down payment is required for the credit purchase of used vehicles, represents the average amount that banks and other lending institutions have been willing to lend buyers toward the purchase of the described vehicle.

The *M.S.R.P.* listed in the *N.A.D.A. Guide* often has differed considerably from the actual sale price of new cars. From the buyer's point of view, the most important characteristic of the M.S.R.P. is that it includes both dealer costs and the dealer's profit margin. Up to a point, the profit margin is negotiable. Buyers should use the actual dealer cost (sometimes referred to as "invoice cost") as their starting point and bargain up from there; you should avoid starting with the M.S.R.P or list price and negotiating down from that. The April auto issue of *Consumer Reports* magazine contains data presenting list price vs. dealer cost for most models. But as recent sales of some cars for more than the M.S.R.P. suggest, when demand for a particular car is strong and supply is limited (by production capacity or other factors), the profit margin may exceed the manufacturer's guidelines as represented by the M.S.R.P.

Dealer Trade-In or Private Sale?

Once you have determined the probable retail value of your present auto, you have the option of trading it in to the dealer or selling it privately. Many people believe they will get more for a car if they sell it to a private buyer rather than to a dealer. In many instances, this will be the case. By selling the car themselves, they absorb the overhead costs that otherwise would accrue to a dealer, and which he would deduct from the price he would allow you on a trade-in.

However, one factor that may make a private sale inadvisable is the mechanical condition of the car. If you are aware that your car is in need of mechanical repairs, a private sale could result in any number of headaches stemming from a buyer's dissatisfaction. A part of dealer costs deducted from a car's dollar value is, in effect, insurance that you will not be bothered by a disgruntled owner.

From an economic viewpoint, the most significant factor in the decision to sell to a private buyer or to a dealer is the difference in price obtained. The older a car is, the smaller the difference between retail and wholesale values. That is, the difference between what a dealer might offer to pay for your car and what you could expect to realize from a private sale generally will be less for older models than for late-model cars. In view of the possible difficulties that can arise from the sale of older cars, as well as the costs in time and inconvenience to the seller, most people probably will be better off to trade in most older-model cars to the dealer.

Trading-in may also have a tax advantage. In most states, you only pay sales tax on the difference between the price of the new car and the trade-in value. For example, if the new car you are purchasing is $25,000 and the dealer is willing to give you $10,000 for your trade-in, you would only be paying sales tax on $15,000. In states with a high sales tax, or when the difference between what you can get for a trade and what you can get in a private sale is small, this tax benefit could make trading in the better choice.

On the other hand, the price difference between private and dealer purchases of *late-model* cars can be substantial. The difference between *Retail* and *Trade-In* amounts listed in the September 2007 *N.A.D.A. Guide* range anywhere from $1,091 for the 2002 Daewoo Lanos to $7,908 for the 2005 Porsche 911 Turbo. These amounts approximate the losses to sellers from sales to dealers (or conversely, potential gains from sales to private buyers) of late-model cars. Moreover, inasmuch as many manufacturer's warranties now apply for 50,000 miles or more and are transferable to subsequent owners, many of the potential liabilities associated with private sales of older cars do not apply to private sales of late-model used cars. The substantial difference in price indicated for retail and wholesale transactions would seem to favor a sale to a private buyer for late-model cars. In the tables on pages 15-49 we have shown in the right-hand column the difference between average retail prices and the average trade-in allowance for the models listed.

If a private sale is contemplated, it should require full cash (or certified bank draft, cashier's check or money order) payment at the time of sale. Do not be tempted to give in to requests for some kind of owner financing if a prospective buyer cannot come up with the money. If a buyer cannot obtain credit elsewhere, the chances are great that he or she lacks the ability to pay. You could end up with no car and no cash, and be forced into costly and time-consuming litigation for repossession of your property.

VIII.

INSURING YOUR VEHICLE

AN insurance policy is a commercial contract, comparable in most respects to any other written business agreement. A policy includes all terms agreed on and may be construed and interpreted, as any other business contract, although insurance contracts are different in that many people may have the same contract (*i.e.*, group insurance), and the terms of the policy may be set by the state. All insurance contracts are essentially wagers—wagers on the part of the insurance company that the premiums collected against a certain happenstance will cover all payouts, and wagers (*premiums*) by the insured persons that they might at some time have an accident so expensive that it would "break" them financially, unless they have sufficient insurance coverage.

The laws governing insurance require that an insurance contract not be entered into as a mere bet, because taking out an insurance policy merely as a gamble on a future event may create a temptation, or *moral hazard*, to bring about the event insured against. As a result, the basic legal requirement for taking out insurance is that it must cover an *insurable interest*, which usually means that the possible loss of whatever is insured would be of pecuniary damage to the insured, and that the insurer is paid a premium in consideration for entering into the contract.

Insurance companies generally are regulated by the states. Most states license insurance companies that do business within their state, regulate the policies they offer, require them to maintain sufficient reserves to pay claims, and require periodic reports on the internal affairs of the company. The attorney general of your state, the reference librarian of your nearest large university or public library, and your state's insurance department are all possible sources of information to learn more about particular insurers and their standing in the industry and within your state. The standing of national companies may vary from state to state and with the type of insurance being purchased (*e.g.*, auto, homeowners, life, etc.).

Insurance generally is sold by "agents," meaning the salesman is acting as an agent for the insurer, or by "brokers," who sometimes are referred to as "independent agents," indicating that they do not work for any one company but rather act as a go-between for multiple insurance companies and their insured clients. Independent agents supposedly work for the consumer rather than an insurance company. However, in legal and regulatory matters many states place the broker on the insurance companies' side, and not on the side of the insured. Many states require insurance companies, agents, and brokers to be licensed to operate within their state.

Once you agree to purchase a policy, you pay the premium to the insurance company and it sends you a written copy of the policy. The policy should be given a thorough going over, to see whether what you got and what you thought you were going to get are one and the same, or close enough for you to be satisfied. The policy should clearly describe what is covered, under what circumstances it is covered, what you need to do to keep the policy in force, what the insurer needs to do if it wishes to cancel or change all or part of the terms of the policy, and what you need to do to file a claim if that should become necessary.

One very important provision is the notification requirement, especially where it involves the possibility of a lawsuit. Most policies that require a company to "indemnify and defend" you, the insured person, also require that you notify the company promptly of any incident that may result in a claim—usually within 30 days of the incident. If you do not do so, the insurance company may legally deny your claim. You should always call your agent about an incident as soon as possible after it happens, and follow the call with a confirmatory letter for which you should get (and keep in a safe place) proof of mailing, such as a certified mail receipt. Once you have reported an incident, start keeping a record of all related phone calls and correspondence with the insurer and any other involved parties.

If you are involved in an incident where there is no apparent injury but a claim could possibly be made at a later date, alert your agent by phone and mail. Even seemingly minor "fender benders" and the like can lead to future claims of physical or psychological injury. At best, there will never be a claim, but this will give your agent the opportunity to get a "release" from the possibly injured person. It will also preserve your insurer's obligation to "indemnify and defend" you if, after 31 days have elapsed, someone decides they really were injured by you, after all.

Whenever the insurance company must defend an action, whether its stake in the proceedings is relatively small or relatively large, it will send its own attorney(s). The insured, however, should not relax simply because an attorney is there, ostensibly representing the insured as well as the company. The insurer usually is primarily interested in settling the suit in the quickest and cheapest way possible in terms of its own involvement. The insured should be interested in those things, too, but also should be looking out for his or her own interests. For example, how will the settlement or legal decision affect your reputation, your finances, and your credit rating? How will it affect your ability to get affordable insurance after the case is settled? (Will it be necessary to admit to negligence or guilt?) If the insurance company's stake is for only a small part of the total settlement, how much will you have to pay out of your own pocket?

It might be worth having your own legal representative at any settlement negotiations. It goes without saying that you have the obligation to help the insurer defend you (and itself) in any action in which the two of you are involved. But if you think the insurance company's interests and your own do not overlap sufficiently for your own peace of mind, your best recourse probably will be to engage your own counsel.

Casualty insurance, which includes auto insurance, covers one's property (including liabilities arising from claims and judgments) and health. It differs from *life insurance*, not only in that most claims are for less than the full amount of the policy, but also in that certain kinds of life insurance (whole life) policies may have an element of savings and investment for the policyholder that casualty insurance does not. Another important difference is that most life insurance salesmen deal with only one company whereas most casualty insurance is sold by independent agents who deal with many companies (although a few casualty companies, such as State Farm Mutual and Allstate, maintain their own network of agents who work exclusively for them). An independent agent should, in effect, do "comparison shopping" on your behalf. However, it is a good idea to get quotations from more than one agent when purchasing or renewing casualty insurance.

In any event, policies should be purchased from strong and reliable companies. State regulation of insurance companies generally ensures that valid claims eventually are paid. However, the savings from purchasing insurance from an "aggressive" (*i.e.*, low-cost) underwriter, who may be more interested in generating additional premium income than retaining customers, may not justify the effort required to collect on a claim. This is more applicable to casualty insurance than life insurance, inasmuch as there often are grounds for disputing casualty losses, but seldom any with respect to life insurance (the insured is either alive or dead).

Most casualty insurance is written by companies that are owned by stockholders, in contrast to mutual companies that are owned and (in theory) controlled by the policyholders.* In general, the major well-established companies are competitive in their rates for basic insurance coverage of any type. This is not to say that it is inexpensive: if you are purchasing coverage for a genuinely significant risk you can expect to pay a significant sum to get it. On the other hand, risks that have a very small probability of generating claims (either because they have a small probability of occurring or are so narrowly defined as to make an enforceable claim difficult) are cheap to insure against.

The latter type of contract tends to be very profitable for underwriters, which means that they can spend more on salesmen's commissions and other marketing expenses. For example, insurance salesmen often will urge you to buy various "add-on" features over and above the basic coverage, such as roadside assistance or reimbursement for car rental while your own auto is being repaired.

To avoid buying coverage that you do not need, you should review all your policies together, to eliminate duplication of coverage. For example, if you have a sound health insurance policy, additional coverage for "medical expenses" for yourself and family members should not be purchased in connection with automobile or homeowners' coverage.† Similarly, if you already have an auto-club membership that covers towing, you don't need roadside assistance insurance.

Auto Insurance Basics

In general, you should have the broadest possible insurance coverage. You should also make sure that anyone else who is authorized to drive your vehicle is properly licensed and qualified to drive under the terms of the policy. You should be thoroughly informed as to the terms of coverage and what may void them, and take care that anyone who is authorized to drive the car also is fully instructed with respect to these matters. This

---

* Policyholders of mutual companies seldom, if ever, assert their legal rights of control over management.

† Some policies do not pay if coverage is duplicated by another policy or entity. If so, it will say so somewhere in the policy. Others will pay only the excess of the cost incurred, essentially taking a "second position" to the primary payor, who exhausts its total contractual obligation owed to the insured, before the other insurer picks up any obligation.

also applies to rented vehicles. Anyone who drives, or even rides in, a vehicle that is not properly insured is running an unacceptable and usually needless risk.

The most widely purchased type of insurance protects the owner of an automobile from claims for injury to persons and for damage to property resulting from legal liability that may arise as a result of an automobile accident. Proof of such insurance for "public liability," covering liability for injury or death to persons, and for "property damage," covering liability for damage to another person's property, generally is required in order to register a motor vehicle for use on public highways and streets. Even the careful driver needs this coverage. As the costs of operating a vehicle and the costs of insuring a vehicle have increased, so too has the number of drivers who are either "underinsured" or driving unregistered, uninsured vehicles while they themselves also are unlicensed—either because they never bothered to get a license or because their right to drive has been revoked due to the number or kind of infractions they have perpetrated as drivers. An accident with an uninsured driver means that only your own insurance stands between you and the full brunt of all bills incurred. Many companies thus offer "uninsured motorist coverage" for this eventuality.

The degree of coverage afforded varies in policies issued by different companies, and the minimum amount of coverage required to register a vehicle varies from state to state. Look for the broadest possible coverage, and make certain that the company under consideration is of high standing, with a favorable record of treating policyholders fairly.

Some states closely regulate automobile insurance premiums. In such states, you should select your insurer on the basis of service and financial standing. On the other hand, if rates vary from company to company, you also should investigate costs. Be sure to examine not only the cost of the particular segment of insurance you are currently looking at, but the cost of the total package. For example, many auto insurance company "packages" are within a few dollars of each other in terms of total premiums for collision, comprehensive, and liability umbrella, but the price for each of those items separately may or may not be competitive with the item-by-item costs of some other insurer.

Most states require you to have a minimum amount of insurance coverage in order to register a vehicle. However, these minimums are usually grossly inadequate. Should you ever be involved in a lawsuit charging you with liability in a car accident, you could find yourself in a court jurisdiction that places no limit on the amount that may be awarded to the victims of an accident. Without adequate insurance, you face the prospect of losing some or all of the wealth that you have accumulated during your lifetime to satisfy a legal judgment. Many individuals have been forced into bankruptcy by such judgments, and recently the trend of the law has been to hold that bankruptcy will not discharge a judgment obtained as a result of an automobile injury.

The mandatory minimums may be as little as $15,000 coverage for death or injury to one person, with a $30,000 aggregate limit of damage for death or injury to all persons to whom the owner becomes liable in a single accident. (Such amounts would be described in the jargon of the industry as "15/30 limits.") The cost of this insurance varies with a number of factors: where you live, the vehicle model, the age, sex, and qualification of the operator, and the principal use of the vehicle. Typically it amounts to roughly $100 to $250 per year for 15/30 limits. The additional premium charged for increasing the amount of coverage is small compared with the increased protection afforded the insured. Increasing the coverage to 100/300 (*i.e.*, $100,000 per person and $300,000 per accident) might only double the premium from what you pay for the statutory minimum.

The limit of the insurance company's liability is that stated in the policy, regardless of the amount of the award; the automobile owner becomes responsible for any liability in excess of that amount. In today's times of high costs for medical and rehabilitation attention and for day-to-day living expenses, financial awards to severely injured victims of automobile accidents easily can reach the hundreds of thousands of dollars. Needless to say, the risk of loss is substantial, and automobile accidents happen even to careful drivers. It is advisable to carry at least 100/300 bodily injury coverage, and persons with substantial wealth or earning potential that could be taken to pay bodily injury awards should carry more.

An alternative way to get higher bodily injury coverage for automobile accidents is with an "umbrella policy" for personal liability. Umbrella policies supplement the liability coverage provided by an insured's existing auto and home insurance. An added advantage is that an umbrella policy's coverage extends beyond bodily injury and property damage. It also covers personal injury for liability arising from claims such as slander, libel, wrongful eviction, and false arrest, and that from serving on the board of a civic, charitable, or religious organization. Since most of the risk is assumed under the primary auto and homeowners policies, a $1 million umbrella policy generally costs less than $200 per year. Some companies will sell you an umbrella policy only if you purchase your primary home and auto insurance from them. In addition, they often require you to carry a minimum of, say, 250/500 bodily injury and $100,000 property damage liability on your auto policy and $300,000 liability on your homeowners policy. Finally, umbrella policies are usually sold with a deductible that ranges from $250 to $1,000.

Protection from liability for injury to or destruction of the property of others through accident, called "property damage coverage," likewise should be included in one's insurance. It is not expensive. The usual minimum coverage is $10,000, for which the annual cost might be roughly $100. Because judgments well in excess of this amount are not uncommon, many individuals might well increase this coverage tenfold to $100,000. As with bodily injury coverage, the premiums do not increase proportionately with the maximum coverage.

In addition to these two highly desirable (and generally mandatory, if the vehicle is to be driven on a public way) types of coverage, most policies also insure against damage to or loss of the automobile itself. Such "collision" coverage usually is subject to a deductible, which is the portion of any claim that the owner must pay himself. Coverage for damage incurred in a collision is costly. It often accounts for well over half of a motorist's auto insurance premium.

If a vehicle is subject to a lien in favor of a lender who financed its purchase, the lender typically will require the owner to carry collision insurance up to the amount of the outstanding balance of the loan. Beyond any such requirement, collision coverage is optional—it is up to the owner to decide whether to buy it. If everyone who is going to drive your car is a careful driver, and you easily could bear the cost of replacing or repairing your car (as might be the case with, say, an older car), the purchase of collision coverage may not be warranted. Of course, if you could not readily afford to replace your car and if the use of the car is nearly essential, you probably cannot afford to be without collision coverage, even if the premium rate is relatively high.

Keep in mind that when your car is damaged, the insurance company will reimburse you based on its assessment of how much it would cost to repair the car. If the repair costs are higher than the value of the car, minus its salvage value, the car is considered to be "totaled." (The expression "totaled" refers to economic damages, not mechanical damages. When a car is "totaled," this does not mean it cannot be repaired; it means that it would cost more to repair it than the car is worth.) In such cases, the company will not repair the car but will pay you its market value. If a car is very old or in very poor condition, and therefore has little market value, relatively minor damages can quickly total it. When this happens, the amount you will be reimbursed may be very small in relation to the premium you must pay for collision coverage. At or near that point, you should drop the collision coverage.

One way to reduce the cost of collision insurance is to increase the amount of the deductible to $500 or even $1,000, from the more usual $250, so that only a very severe accident will result in a claim for collision damage. The downside is that you will be responsible for paying the repair costs of most minor mishaps. However, consider the possibility that you might end up doing so even if you do not have a large deductible. Many people choose not to put in claims for relatively minor damages, even if their insurance would cover them, because some insurance companies will raise your premiums after you make even one claim, or drop your coverage altogether if they decide there have been too many claims *of any sort*.

In the past, collision premiums decreased substantially as a car aged, because the value of the car that the insurance company was liable for decreased. But now that the prices of new cars have risen markedly, the prices of older cars are also relatively high. Thus the potential financial loss to an insurance company providing collision coverage does not decrease much as a car ages, and, additionally, the cost of each collision increases along with the cost of the car; consequently, collision premiums do not decrease much either.

Companies now issue what is known as a "comprehensive policy," which gives protection primarily against loss from fire and theft but also includes protection for loss due to practically any other hazard (except collision), including windstorms, tornadoes, hailstorms, floods, acts of vandalism, etc. The additional cost of such comprehensive coverage over the premium for plain fire and theft coverage is nominal. Insurance companies grade geographical locations according to the number and severity of the accidents occurring in each. These factors determine the rate for any single location.

"Uninsured motorists" coverage pays if you are injured by a hit-and-run driver or a driver who does not have auto insurance." "Underinsured" coverage protects you from drivers whose insurance may not be sufficient to cover your claim. Some states require specific minimum amounts of such coverage, but these amounts are often inadequate. Raising coverage beyond the statutory limits to, say, 100/300 is not very expensive and adds substantial protection. This coverage normally does not cover damage to your vehicle or protect the other driver.

"Medical payments" coverage pays for medical costs for you or for others injured in an accident while driving or riding in your auto, or you or family members if you are struck by an auto while walking or riding in another auto. The coverage pays regardless of who is at fault. The cost is minimal, but such coverage may duplicate coverage that you already have through other health insurance or disability insurance. "Personal injury" protection reimburses you for lost wages if you are injured, and for the wages of people who are hired to assist you during recovery (*e.g.* the costs of in-home care). Many states require you to buy a minimum amount of coverage; whether raising those limits makes sense depends on the existing coverage provided by your health and disability policies.

A number of states now have "no-fault" automobile insurance statutes. There are substantial differences in these laws among the states, but the common feature is that a victim of an automobile accident who suffers bodily injury must recover his financial loss from his own insurance company rather than from another party. No-fault statutes in some states also apply to property damage losses. The no-fault feature applies to losses of specified amounts or less. Recovery for losses above these amounts must be made under the usual provisions of insurance and law. Every insured should learn if there are no-fault laws in his state, and should consult his insurance agent about them if there are such laws.

Read your policy and thoroughly familiarize yourself with its terms. Failure to do so may have serious consequences. All too frequently, individuals are surprised to discover that the particular situation in which they find themselves is not covered by their policy, either because there was no protection against it originally or because they, or someone acting for them, did something to invalidate the coverage or failed to do something required, and the policy has therefore been voided in that particular case. As noted earlier, it is especially important to promptly notify your insurance company in writing when an incident occurs, or the company may deny your claim. Usually you must do this within 30 days, but check the notification requirement in your policy to see what its terms are.

With regard to rental vehicle insurance, car rental businesses offer insurance on their vehicles, which may or may not duplicate coverage of your own policy. Before renting a vehicle, check with your own agent to find out whether or not you need to purchase the insurance the car rental agent is obligated by law to offer you. Since the rental agency's insurance usually is a daily surcharge, it may amount to a substantial sum. If you carefully read the tiny, light-colored print on the back of any such contract, you may find that it says your own insurance company will take "first position" in any accident, meaning that your own insurance will pay all the costs until that coverage is exhausted, after which the rental insurance will begin paying the excess. You also may find that the car rental company's total liability will be limited to a relatively small amount.

In general, whether or not you will be driving underinsured or uninsured if you fail to sign up for the rental agency's insurance will depend in part on how far the type and purpose of the rented vehicle differs from what your own insurance covers. For example, it is more likely that your existing automobile and homeowner policies will cover you if you rent an automobile than if you rent, say, a U-Haul truck. If you contemplate renting a vehicle, it is advisable to have a copy of your policy and proof of insurance with you, especially if you wish to rent when you are outside your home state. Carry your insurance agent's telephone number with you when you travel, and call ahead to find out what you will need to have in order to rent the vehicle you want.

Any written notification of changes in a policy, and all new or renewed policies, ought to be reviewed thoroughly. The written copy you receive via the mail is your notification of change to your policy; if you fail to read such notifications, they are nevertheless in force and you will be deemed to have read and agreed to them. By knowing what is in your policy, you are less likely to be surprised by not having coverage you expected to have when you need it.

Some companies offer discounts and credits that, although not huge, still are helpful. Discounts are given for having all vehicles insured with the same company, and credits are given to drivers who have completed certified safe-driving courses. Discounts may also be available for vehicles

Table 11
AVERAGE EXPENDITURE FOR AUTO INSURANCE, 2004

Nationwide average expenditure	$838
Average premium for full coverage	
(liability, comprehensive, and collision)	$960
Liability coverage	$499
Collision coverage	$314
Comprehensive coverage	$147

National average outlays for privately-owned passenger vehicles in 2004.
Source: Insurance Information Institute.

---

with certain safety or antitheft devices, and for students with good grades. Be sure to request a complete list of all available discounts to determine which ones you might be eligible for.

According to the Insurance Information Institute, the average person spent $838 on auto insurance in 2004 (the latest year available). This average is affected by a number of factors, including the underlying rate structure, the amount and type of coverage purchased, the deductibles, the types of vehicles insured, the distribution of driver characteristics, and state regulations. In 2004, those who purchased "full" coverage (that is, a combination of liability, collision, and comprehensive insurance) paid $960, on average, in premiums. (See Table 11.)

Where to Find Help

The National Insurance Consumer Helpline, (800) 942-4242 or (800) 331-9146, is a toll-free consumer information telephone service sponsored by three major insurance industry trade associations. The associations represent all segments of insurance, including life, health, and home and auto (property/casualty) insurance companies. Trained personnel and licensed agents are available to assist consumers in three important areas. They answer a wide range of questions about various insurance matters, are able to refer consumer complaints to appropriate sources, and will send consumer brochures upon request. The Helpline operates from 8:00 a.m. to 8:00 p.m. EST, Monday through Friday.

Table 12 provides a list of phone numbers where you can reach your state insurance department. Those with internet access can find a link to their state insurance department's website at www.naic.org/state_web_map.htm. The site is provided by the National Association of Insurance Commissioners.

Table 12
STATE INSURANCE DEPARTMENTS

AK	907-269-7900	KY	800-595-6053	NY	800-342-3736
AL	334-269-3550	LA	800-259-5300	OH	800-686-1526
AR	800-282-9134	MA	617-521-7794	OK	800-522-0071
AZ	602-364-3100	MD	410-468-2090	OR	503-947-7980
CA	800-927-4357	ME	207-624-8401	PA	877-881-6388
CO	303-894-7490	MI	877-999-6442	RI	401-222-2223
CT	860-297-3800	MN	800-657-3602	SC	803-737-6160
DC	202-727-8000	MO	573-751-1927	SD	605-773-3563
DE	800-282-8611	MS	601-359-3569	TN	615-741-2218
FL	850-413-3140	MT	406-444-2040	TX	800-252-7031
GA	404-656-2070	NC	800-546-5664	UT	800-439-3805
HI	808-586-2790	ND	701-328-2440	VA	804-371-9741
IA	877-955-1212	NE	877-564-7323	VT	802-828-3301
ID	800-721-3272	NH	800-852-3416	WA	360-725-7080
IL	866-445-5364	NJ	800-446-7467	WI	800-236-8517
IN	317-232-2385	NM	800-947-4722	WV	888-879-9842
KS	800-432-2484	NV	775-687-4270	WY	800-438-5768

IX.

YOUR COST RECORD

KEEPING an accurate record of the costs of owning and operating an automobile is the only way you can determine how much your car is costing you, and whether the costs of keeping your present car are greater or less than they would be for a new car. The ledgers that follow this section provide space for entering virtually all car-related outlays. The discussion below provides instruction in how to keep the ledgers.

Keeping the Ledgers

At the beginning and end of each month, record the odometer mileage in the spaces provided. If it is necessary or desirable to monitor each operator's use of the car, or if business use of the car must be distinguished from personal use, beginning and ending odometer readings also should be recorded in the appropriate columns. Business or other tax-deductible use and expenditures can be indicated by checking the appropriate boxes. At the end of each month, the percent of each operator's use or the percentage of business use of the vehicle can be calculated by dividing total mileage for each operator or for business use (from the "Odometer Readings" column) by the total monthly mileage recorded for the vehicle.

Where several operators share the costs of maintaining the car, or in cases where it may be desirable for younger drivers to be aware of the portion of costs for which they are responsible (or where parents may require that they contribute to paying some of those costs), their percent of the total mileage can be multiplied by total monthly costs (recorded on the summary page) to determine the corresponding dollar amount of monthly costs. The sum of each operator's recorded expenditures can be subtracted from his or her share of costs to determine what amount ought to be paid or refunded.

The annual dollar cost of business use of a car can be calculated similarly. In the box under "Tax-Related Items" on the summary page, each month enter the business mileage and related expenses that have been recorded in the monthly ledgers. At the end of the year, in the box headed "Recapitulation," enter on line (1) the total annual mileage on the vehicle (from the "Annual Totals" line in the summary table). On line (2) enter the amount from "Grand Total" in the summary table. On line (4) enter total business mileage from the "Totals" line in the "Tax-Related Items" box. Divide line (4) by line (1) and enter the quotient (percent business mileage) on line (5). This percentage represents the proportion of use attributable to business purposes. Approximate corresponding business costs can be calculated by multiplying the amount on line (2) by line (5). However, adjustments must be made if business or non-business expenses unrelated to actual maintenance and operation of the vehicle are much larger or smaller than average—say, if the tolls and parking were nearly all business related. These items should be closely monitored, and monthly business expenses recorded in the box on the summary page.

Current Federal tax regulations require that an accurate log of business-related and personal mileage be kept as documentation of business and personal use of a vehicle. But tax regulations have been subject to frequent changes. In addition to keeping a careful ledger, it is highly advisable also to keep all related receipts. The more complete your documentation, the better will be any defense of deductions relating to business use of a car, or, if you are subject to taxation of fringe-benefit income related to your personal use of a business vehicle, the level of your income tax liability.

Implications of Changes in Component Costs

Throughout the life of a car, several of the cost components should remain relatively constant. Among them are such expenses as gasoline, oil, accessories, garaging, parking, tolls, etc. The amounts spent for each of these items are easily recorded in the appropriate columns in the monthly ledgers as they occur. Other things being equal, monthly fluctuations in these costs will for the most part simply reflect variations in mileage driven.

Of course, expenditures for gasoline will be proportionally greater for cars that get poor mileage than for cars that get good mileage—but this will not be reflected in the ledgers so long as they are kept for only one vehicle. If your family operates more than one car, it will be useful to keep a separate account of costs for each vehicle. How much differences in gas mileage may contribute to total cost differences between two cars then can be ascertained by (1) dividing the total cost of gasoline by the total mileage driven for each vehicle, and (2) subtracting the smaller result from the larger. This result is the cost difference per mile between the two cars.

Miles per gallon (M.P.G.) results can be monitored monthly by dividing monthly total mileage by total gallons purchased. Rapid decreases in M.P.G.

that cannot be accounted for by, say, a switch from mainly highway driving to mainly city driving usually indicate that a car has a mechanical problem. Early detection of such problems can save costly repairs that might result later on if the problem is allowed to worsen.

There are several large costs that can vary considerably from year to year—and these have important cost-saving implications. The most variable "big expense" items include depreciation, insurance, and repairs and maintenance.

Repairs and maintenance usually become a larger cost item after several years of driving, partly because many car owners defer needed repairs in the apparent belief that when they trade in their car after four or five years, they will save the cost of repairs. But either the original owner will absorb the cost of repair work indirectly (through a higher outlay for the new car), or a subsequent buyer will pay less for the used auto—and then pay the cost of the repairs himself. Often the second owner's cost of repairs may be higher than would have been the case if the work had been done when a problem was first discovered. The practice of neglecting needed repairs may be more costly to both original and subsequent owners than if repairs were made when needed.

Repair and maintenance costs ought to be recorded in the appropriate column in the monthly ledger, and repair orders and receipts ought to be retained (in the event that the repair is not satisfactorily made). If repair costs do increase to a level (and continue there) where costs are about the same (or exceed) what they would be for a similar new car, then it is time to trade in.

Also, on a cost-per-mile basis, insurance costs usually tend to decrease as a car ages (because the car is worth less). Here again, you can save money by keeping a car as long as possible.

Calculating Depreciation Costs

We have included in the monthly ledgers under "ownership costs" a column for depreciation. **Depreciation is not the same as your monthly car payment.** It represents the dollar amount by which your car decreased in value during that time period—which may differ greatly from what your loan payment may be. It is a measure that must be incorporated into an accurate account of actual car costs. However, depreciation often is ignored by car owners and auto salesmen, who erroneously equate the monthly

Chart 3
**AVERAGE RETAIL PRICE OF USED VEHICLES
AS A PERCENTAGE OF M.S.R.P. FOR ALL MODELS, 2002-2006**
(September 2007)

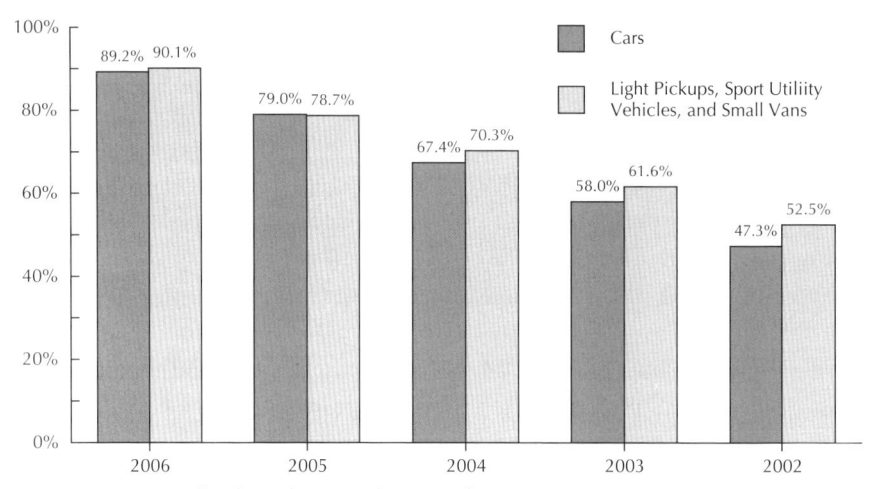

Year	Cars	Light Pickups, Sport Utility Vehicles, and Small Vans
2006	89.2%	90.1%
2005	79.0%	78.7%
2004	67.4%	70.3%
2003	58.0%	61.6%
2002	47.3%	52.5%

Source: *N.A.D.A. Official Used Car Guide*, September 2007.
Note: Data averaged over all regions.

payment with the ownership cost of a car.

Admittedly, any depreciation estimate will be only an informed guess, since no one knows exactly how much dollar value a car will lose over a given period of time. But some estimates can be made more accurately than others. A rule of thumb is that automobiles typically lose about half their value during the first four years. Even brief reference to the tables on pages 15-49 shows that some vehicles lose much less of their dollar value than this rule suggests, and some lose much more. According to the tables, in 2007, 2003 models were selling for anywhere from 34 percent to 96 percent of their original M.S.R.P.

The estimates of average used car retail prices as percentages of M.S.R.P. for all models for 2002-2006 (shown in Chart 3) probably exaggerate somewhat the retained values of late-model cars, especially for the first year. But they still indicate that many vehicles can be expected to depreciate substantially during the first couple of years. Of course, some cars depreciate more quickly than others, as indicated in the tables on pages 15-49. A more accurate estimate of depreciation for a particular car might be derived from those tables. An even more accurate procedure would involve checking the average retail prices listed in the *N.A.D.A. Official Used Car Guide* each month, but probably few owners will want to go to that trouble. Whatever method is used to estimate depreciation, that amount—not the car payment—ought to be entered in the ledgers as part of ownership costs.

Amortize Interest Costs

If you purchase a car on credit, for practical purposes interest payments on the car loan ought to be included in ownership costs, even though technically they are not (they represent the cost of borrowing money). Monthly interest ought to be entered in the ledger in the same column as depreciation for the duration of the loan. Table 13 shows monthly interest amounts per $1,000 of loan value for a 48-month loan at various rates. You can get similar tables for loans with different maturities and interest rates on the AIER website at http://www.aier.org/research/calcs.php.

Table 13
MONTHLY INTEREST PER 1,000 AT SELECTED RATES

Month	4.0%	4.5%	5.0%	5.5%	6.0%	6.5%	7.0%
1	$3.33	$3.75	$4.17	$4.58	$5.00	$5.42	$5.83
2	3.27	3.68	4.09	4.50	4.91	5.32	5.73
3	3.20	3.61	4.01	4.41	4.81	5.22	5.62
4	3.14	3.53	3.93	4.33	4.72	5.12	5.51
5	3.08	3.46	3.85	4.24	4.63	5.02	5.41
6	3.01	3.39	3.77	4.15	4.53	4.92	5.30
7	2.95	3.32	3.69	4.06	4.44	4.81	5.19
8	2.88	3.24	3.61	3.98	4.34	4.71	5.08
9	2.81	3.17	3.53	3.89	4.25	4.61	4.97
10	2.75	3.10	3.45	3.80	4.15	4.51	4.86
11	2.68	3.02	3.37	3.71	4.05	4.40	4.75
12	2.62	2.95	3.28	3.62	3.96	4.30	4.64
13	2.55	2.87	3.20	3.53	3.86	4.19	4.52
14	2.48	2.80	3.12	3.44	3.76	4.09	4.41
15	2.42	2.72	3.04	3.35	3.66	3.98	4.30
16	2.35	2.65	2.95	3.26	3.56	3.87	4.18
17	2.28	2.57	2.87	3.17	3.46	3.76	4.07
18	2.21	2.50	2.79	3.07	3.36	3.66	3.95
19	2.15	2.42	2.70	2.98	3.26	3.55	3.83
20	2.08	2.35	2.62	2.89	3.16	3.44	3.72
21	2.01	2.27	2.53	2.80	3.06	3.33	3.60
22	1.94	2.19	2.45	2.70	2.96	3.22	3.48
23	1.87	2.11	2.36	2.61	2.86	3.11	3.36
24	1.80	2.04	2.27	2.51	2.75	3.00	3.24
25	1.73	1.96	2.19	2.42	2.65	2.88	3.12
26	1.66	1.88	2.10	2.32	2.55	2.77	3.00
27	1.59	1.80	2.01	2.23	2.44	2.66	2.88
28	1.52	1.72	1.93	2.13	2.34	2.54	2.75
29	1.45	1.64	1.84	2.03	2.23	2.43	2.63
30	1.38	1.57	1.75	1.94	2.12	2.31	2.51
31	1.31	1.49	1.66	1.84	2.02	2.20	2.38
32	1.24	1.41	1.57	1.74	1.91	2.08	2.25
33	1.17	1.33	1.48	1.64	1.80	1.96	2.13
34	1.10	1.25	1.39	1.54	1.69	1.85	2.00
35	1.03	1.16	1.30	1.44	1.58	1.73	1.87
36	0.96	1.08	1.21	1.34	1.47	1.61	1.74
37	0.88	1.00	1.12	1.24	1.36	1.49	1.61
38	0.81	0.92	1.03	1.14	1.25	1.37	1.48
39	0.74	0.84	0.94	1.04	1.14	1.25	1.35
40	0.67	0.76	0.85	0.94	1.03	1.13	1.22
41	0.59	0.67	0.75	0.84	0.92	1.00	1.09
42	0.52	0.59	0.66	0.73	0.81	0.88	0.96
43	0.45	0.51	0.57	0.63	0.69	0.76	0.82
44	0.37	0.42	0.47	0.53	0.58	0.63	0.69
45	0.30	0.34	0.38	0.42	0.46	0.51	0.55
46	0.22	0.25	0.29	0.32	0.35	0.38	0.41
47	0.15	0.17	0.19	0.21	0.23	0.25	0.28
48	0.08	0.09	0.10	0.11	0.12	0.13	0.14
Total	83.79	94.57	105.41	116.31	127.28	138.32	149.42

APPENDIX: USEFUL LINKS

New and Used Prices, Information and Reviews
National Automobile Dealer Association
　www.nadaguides.com
Edmunds.com
　www.edmunds.com
Kelly Blue Book
　www.kbb.com
National Highway Traffic Safety Administration
　www.nhtsa.gov
CARFAX
　www.carfax.com
AutoCheck
　www.autocheck.com

Hybrid Tax Credit
U.S. Department of Energy
　www.fueleconomy.gov
Internal Revenue Service
　www.irs.gov

Insurance
National Association of Insurance Commissioners
　www.naics.com
Insurance Information Institute
　www.iii.org/individuals/auto/

Leasing
The Federal Reserve offers a free brochure "Keys to Vehicle Leasing."
　www.federalreserve.gov/pubs/leasing

Financing
The Federal Trade Commission publishes a helpful brochure, "Understanding Vehicle Financing."
　www.ftc.gov/autos

*Monthly Ledger
and
Annual Summary*

Month of _____ 20____   **OPERATING**

Vehicle _____

Driver & Date	✓	Odometer Readings	Gasoline ✓ Gals. Amount	Oil ✓ Qts. Amount	✓ Parking	✓ Tolls	Tax Deductible Expenses & Mileage Amount	Mileage
		/						
		/						
		/						
		/						
		/						
		/						
		/						
		/						
		/						
		/						
		/						
		/						
		/						
		/						
		/						
		/						
		/						
		/						
		/						
		/						
		/						
		/						
		/						
		/						
		/						
		/						
		/						
		/						
		/						
		/						
		/						
Totals								

✓ Check box if item is deductible as a business expense.

EXPENDITURES

Ending Odometer Reading: _____
Beginning Odometer Reading: _____
Total Mileage: _____

Date	Maintenance & Repairs Description	Amount	Accessories Description	Amount
Totals				

OWNERSHIP COSTS

Taxes & Fees (license, registration, inspection, excise, etc.)			Insurance			Estimated Depreciation
Date	Description	Amount	Date	Description	Amount	Amount
Totals						

20___ ANNUAL SUMMARY

Month	Mileage	Gasoline	Oil	Maintenance & Repairs	Accessories	Parking Fees	Tolls	Estimated Depreciation	Insurance	Taxes & Fees	Monthly Totals
Annual Totals											

Total Costs

TAX-RELATED ITEMS

Month	Business Mileage	Deductible Expenses
Totals		

RECAPITULATION

(1) Total mileage: _____

(2) Total costs: _____

(3) Annual cost per mile: _____
    (line 2 ÷ line 1)

(4) Total business mileage: _____

(5) Percent business mileage: _____
    (line 4 ÷ line 1)

(6) Business costs: _____
    (line 2 × line 5)

To buy publications or find out more about
American Institute for Economic Research please contact us at:

American Institute for Economic Research
250 Division Street
Post Office Box 1000
Great Barrington, MA 01230
Phone: (413) 528-1216
Fax: (413) 528-0103

E-mail: aierpubs@aier.org

On-line: www.aier.org